The Game of School

Observations of a Long-haul Teacher

by

Robert L. Tripp

EXTENDED VISION PRESS, RESTON, VIRGINIA

Ashleigh Brilliant Pot-Shots used by permission of the author, Ashleigh Brilliant, 117 West Valerio St., Santa Barbara, CA 93101.

Printed in the United States of America.

Produced by AAH Graphics, Inc. (703) 933-6210

ISBN: 0-9636807-0-6

Library of Congress Catalog Card Number 93-90446
Tripp, Robert L.
The Game of School
Reston, VA: Extended Vision Press

Theme/Premise:

"If you give a hungry man food, he will stop being hungry. If you show him how to grow his own food, he'll never go hungry."

—Ancient Chinese Proverb

POT-SHOTS NO. 1123.
Ashleigh
Brilliant

I WAS
EDUCATED ONCE,

AND
IT TOOK ME
YEARS
TO GET OVER IT.

© BRILLIANT ENTERPRISES 1977

Dedication

To Mary, without whose incredible help
and unfailing patience with me,
this book would never have been completed.

To David, Karen and Sarah—
always wonderful, supportive and helpful.

To the several thousand students
I worked with over the 30 years.
Without doubt, it was they
who made being a teacher worthwhile.

To the good teachers:
they understand.

Acknowledgments

A number of practitioners and writers in the fields of education and psychology have influenced my thinking and my teaching. I want to acknowledge their help. Not that I necessarily agree with everything they have said; nor do I want to make them responsible for how I have used their ideas—that is my doing alone. But their insight and vision enormously helped me develop as a person, helped me become the kind of teacher I tried to be and helped me in the development of my own ideas. They include: Sylvia Ashton-Warner, Eric Berne, James Comer, John Dewey, Paulo Freire, Edgar Z. Friedenberg, Sigmund Freud, William Glasser, Paul Goodman, Thomas Gordon, James Herndon, John Holt, Ivan D. Illich, Arthur T. Jersild, Herbert Kohl, Jonathon Kozol, Abraham Maslow, A.S. Neill, Neil Postman, Alvin F. Poussaint, Ted Sizer, Alfred North Whitehead.

These people influenced me through their books and, in a few cases, workshops of theirs I attended or conversations I have had with them. For their help toward my developing my own vantage point, for the freedom to adapt and build upon their ideas and insight, thanks to them all. It is comforting and exhilarating to know that I am in good company in my quest for good education.

Not only do I a feel a connection with people going back at least as far as Dewey and Freud, but I feel a connection with (and comfort from) people out there right now developing ideas and strategies to make education what it ought to and could be—people like Robert Tierney with his work on collaborative evaluation, people in the various writing project programs around the country, such as the Bay Area Writing Project, and people in the co-operative learning movement, such as David W. Johnson, Roger T. Johnson and Edythe Johnson Holubec.

Many thanks to these friends and former colleagues who were of special help and support to me as a teacher and in writing this book:

Dave Allardice	Carol Bradley
Don Archer	Sally Carter
Bonnie Becker	Betty Chilton
Curry Belfield	Trudy Cunningham

Pam Curtis	Alta Newman
Nick Econopouly	Ting-yi Oei
Jacqui Ferguson	Dolores Paskal
Marie Griffin	Mary Roots
Marge Hope	Morris Saxe
Bruce Hunt	Bernie Schneider
Dan Jackson	Fran Simcich
Mitch Karro	Carl Stephens
John Malone	Bob Venning

Many thanks to these folks for kindly reading parts of the manuscript and offering helpful comments:

Edie Bluske	Fran Tellner
Chuck Cascio	David Tripp
Angela Econopouly	Karen Tripp
Nick Econopouly	Sarah Tripp
Josh Harwood	Colin Walker
Bruce Hunt	Ray Wilkins
Linda Norman	Olga Wright
Ellen Orleans	Richard Wright
Ned Orleans	

Finally, special thanks to Ann and Steve Hunter, my editor and producer, who were helpful and supportive beyond the call of duty, and to Eva and Colin Barrett, who introduced me to Ann and Steve.

Robert L. Tripp, Reston, Virginia

Contents

The Premise:
No Game

1

The What and Why of This Book

American schools need changing. Everyone seems to agree.

But most proposals for education reform in this country head off in the wrong direction. They will change form but not substance. We do not need more hours of school every day and more days of school every year *with schools as they now are*. We do not need to train students to memorize information just to spit it back on tests. That gives the appearance that they are being educated when they are not. This pretense of learning lies at the heart of student boredom and cynicism. Student boredom and cynicism leads to students spending their time and energy figuring out how to cut classes, learning to cheat and wiggling out of doing school work.

Pretense, boredom, and cynicism are central elements in the destructive *game* that is the norm in American public high schools.

The long-haul teacher

I wrote this book because my 30 years as a teacher convinces me that our schools do need change—serious, radical change. We need schools that actively and meaningfully engage students in the process of their own learning. We need schools where the atmosphere is constructive, not destructive. There must be a connection between academic pursuit and the world outside for which school is supposed to prepare students. Students also deserve to discover the joy and value of growing and learning as a life-long activity for its own sake. Schools can do all this and teach job skills too.

Thus, this book is an insider's critique of public high schools today, and a proposal to improve them through short and long term changes.

I was a regular, long-haul teacher. This is important to stress because in the cacophony about schools in recent years, the voice of the ordinary classroom teacher is seldom heard. I was a high school social studies teacher in three separate blocks of time, at the beginning, middle and end of my teaching career, a total of 18 years. In between these stints I taught for a year in England, directed a federally-funded project in an urban junior high school, ran a graduate teacher education program and worked in a school system human relations department—a total of 30 years in the business. But I was always a teacher, and the heart and soul of my odyssey as an educator was students.

The game

The game may not be obvious to the casual observer. An outsider visiting a public high school today would probably not see the scenes of cruelty found in *Tom Brown's School Days*.[1] Today's horrors and abuses are not physical punishment and dark, dim classrooms. The horror of today's game comes from the subtle cruelty of environments and relationships that make serious learning—and the subsequent joy of learning—nearly impossible. This is as true for suburban high schools with relatively affluent, predominately white student bodies as it is for inner city schools with relatively poor, predominately African-American student bodies.

Schools have learned how to mask what is going on. Though retaining their institutional look, most contemporary high schools *are* cleaner and brighter than they once were. Students *appear* to have more flexibility in what and how they study. They seem to have greater freedom of movement within the school than they had a generation or so ago.

Teachers and administrators use jargon that deceives. To the unsuspecting outsider it may appear that creating a positive learning environment and making sure kids learn material that is useful are their primary goals. Don't bet on it.

In *Games People Play*[2], Eric Berne described and analyzed the kinds of psychological destructive behavior that far too many people exhibit. He emphasized that the coy games so often played by people for hidden or unconscious ends get in the way of real feelings and of meeting real needs. He noted that in the end these games hurt those who start them as well as those who are the intended targets.

4

Such games go on constantly in schools: among the teachers and administrators, between them and students and, partly as a consequence, among the students. This is why for most students school is a game. The successful ones learn to play it well. If they learn anything more substantive, that is a fortunate by-product or accident.

Far too many teachers and administrators willingly play the game. Far too many teachers and administrators do not like kids. Often, they are rigid and cruel when dealing with kids. They wound and kill the natural curiosity and enthusiasm of kids. There is a tendency for teachers to be defensive and to deny how things really are. Much of the fault for this lies in how the school system (*the system*) operates: what it does and does not encourage by way of teacher behavior and values. Much of the fault also lies in the poor training most teachers receive, and in the lack of congruence between their training and the demands of daily life in schools. It is fair to say that teaching has tended to attract people who are not risk-takers, people who want things set, smooth and secure—a big mistake. Teachers who won't take risks and test out the world can't help students do it, either. Yet if students are not encouraged to test out the world, how can they grow and learn?

The main function of school

The faults in the system of public education make me angry. Here we see an institution that, in general, is satisfied to educate kids at the lowest level of learning and growth; an institution that tends to stifle rather than encourage thinking and creativity in teachers as well as in students. The main function of this faulty system is teaching kids how to survive a gauntlet of classes and teachers and administrators.

Making this harsh judgement hurts. After all, schools were a huge part of my life for a long time. And I know they are complex places. On the one hand they do great damage, and miss many opportunities to truly educate students. On the other hand, most of them try to do the best they can *given the constraints under which they operate*.

Teachers work hard. Often they are not recognized for their successes. Many of the problems of schools are beyond the scope of what the classroom teacher or the school administrator can solve. Even so, it is vital that we understand what really happens in school if we are serious about making public education work the way we want it to work.

Ah, but there's the rub! How *do* we want it to work? Do we all want the same things? Obviously, not. Beyond assuming that everyone needs the three R's of "reading, writing and 'rithmetic," there is not much agreement on what schools should do, let alone can do, as they now are structured.

People use the phrase "good education" all the time. But they almost never say what that phrase means. This makes no sense. Unless we define what we mean by good education, we have no clear and firm premise to work from in analyzing the schools and proposing changes. The myriad of proposals and gimmicks that have been suggested and tried usually fall on deaf ears or fail because they are not part of a coherent philosophical framework. Any particular idea must be tested against such a framework to see if it is valid or not. This book provides the necessary philosophical structure with a thorough discussion of what I mean by good education.

What is the primary purpose of our public high schools? It should be to educate young people to be thinking, reasoning, questioning, caring, aware citizens who acquire knowledge—information—*in the context of this purpose.* Instead, it seems to be to jam as many isolated, often unrelated pieces of information down students' throats as possible, so they can do well on tests and above all give the appearance of having learned.

Proposals for change

My proposals for change require schools with certain characteristics that are largely lacking today. Schools must be alive, exciting places where students *want* to come. Schools need a loving, inviting environment. Students must be treated as whole human beings who *want* to learn and grow, and who seek adult help and guidance in the process. Schools must be grounded in intellectual rigor. They must play a significant role in nurturing students. In school, students should develop a lifelong love of learning, the desire to intelligently question authority and each other, and a genuine caring for their fellow human beings. Teachers and administrators must not see kids as adversaries. Kids are younger intelligent people who are in school to be helped, not controlled and manipulated. Schools must be a vital force in developing the aware, involved citizenry that, as Jefferson understood, is necessary in a democracy.

Citizen enlightenment and involvement have been lacking. Slick television ads sway vast numbers of people. Low voter turnout makes a mockery of election day. We resist dealing with or even acknowledging serious social and economic problems. However, the 1992 presidential election may have opened the door to positive change. People spoke out forcefully on many issues, not only on the economy. And voter turnout was up. President Clinton and Vice-President Gore have stressed the importance of redesigning our system of education to encourage lifelong learning and to prepare for many changes in jobs and careers. They have stressed as well the importance of inclusion—of involving *everyone* in the United States in its life and promise. These notions are central to my proposals. Schools must be for *all* kids, not just for the ones who fit certain ideas of what a student is. And changing schools must be the job of *all* people, students and others, who wish to be a part of the process.

We need citizens who genuinely care about the quality of life in this society, who are enlightened and question. Massive unsolved problems threaten the very existence of the nation. Racism, sexism and homophobia are still with us. Poverty is more widespread today than it was a dozen years ago. Homelessness is a shameful reality. The very infrastructure of this country is wobbling. There is the threat of ecological disaster. Along with the exciting changes of recent years in Eastern Europe, the former Soviet Union, South Africa and elsewhere there have emerged more forcefully than ever dangerous and destructive ethnic, racial and religious conflicts. The possibility of nuclear holocaust has not ended. The technological genie is out of the bottle. We must learn how to manage that genie, and soon, or we will be engulfed by it in ways yet undreamed of.

Though the election of Clinton and Gore has brought a ray of hope, there remain much citizen skepticism and student alienation. This pessimism partly reflects what is and is not happening in schools. Too much time is spent on trivia, busywork and the appearance of learning, and too little time helping young people see the importance *for them* of being questioning citizens, actively involved in the life of the nation and world. But active, questioning citizens are exactly what we must have if we are to take advantage of the new possibilities that are opening.

A decent break for all kids

My analysis of schools and learning comes largely from my experiences teaching in middle class schools with majority white student bodies. It might therefore be argued that my suggestions apply mainly to white, middle class, affluent kids who can afford the "luxury" of what I advocate. This is not so. My critique and proposals for change are as valid for African-American inner city kids, or poor rural white kids, as they are for all the others. Many inner city kids, especially, live in such a chaotic, destructive world that some people believe their only chance lies in attending schools that force them to learn. Partly, this is because there is a negative image of a groovy, not-very-orderly school with a "do your own thing" environment. This carryover from the late 1960's and early 1970's still exists to some extent in many high schools today. It is ruinously destructive, and a contributing factor to why even affluent white kids turn off school. This is not what I advocate. I do not believe in a laissez-faire, "do your own thing" approach to learning. But I do not believe in turning schools into military camps either.

Although I taught in middle class, predominately white high schools, these schools included a large number of students from nonwhite and poor families. My perceptions and ideas developed while working with students from diverse backgrounds.

Moreover, I had significant contact with poor and nonwhite students through other jobs held during the 30 years I was a teacher: when I was a supervisor of student teachers; as coordinator of a federally funded education project; and as a human relations specialist. In these jobs, I have discussed my ideas with students, teachers and parents. Many of them share my perceptions about what is good education.

Kids need a coherent, orderly framework where they understand what is going on. But if you just clobber kids over the head and force them to learn, the best you can hope for is that they will pass tests that make it *look* like they have learned. They will not, however, really have learned and grown. They will not make the kinds of connections that bring about true learning. *All* kids must be treated with dignity and honesty. They need a genuine opportunity to test out ideas for themselves and explore the world themselves. Then they are more likely to connect that world with their academic pursuits. Inner city black kids respond just as positively as do other kids to being taken seriously and to being encouraged to take charge of their own learning. Just like all kids, inner city kids respond positively to the nurturing, no-game environment I advocate. The chaos and economic deprivation of inner city kids' backgrounds sometimes may require more patience of teachers. But with patience and love these kids, too, will find effective ways to learn and grow.

Of course, not everyone will agree with me. Still, I am confident that my approach will help inner city kids finally get a decent break. I have been aware of racism in this country for 49 years—since I was in the 7th grade in a racially and ethnically mixed junior high school in San Francisco in 1944. As a citizen and a human being, exposing and opposing racism has been a major concern of my life. As a teacher I helped kids understand, expose and oppose racism, and I have pushed strongly for a multi-cultural curriculum that excludes no one.

It is, therefore, vitally important to me that my ideas about education be understood to have relevance for kids from *all* backgrounds. It cannot be otherwise. The very essence of my concept of good education is that we develop a useful school system for *all* kids.

Analyzing public schools and proposing major, radical changes in them are huge topics. A complete analysis would involve a full understanding of the social, political and economic factors that have an impact on schools and that provide the context for public education. While these larger factors play a role, my critique focuses on how public high schools operate. How do teachers and students function? What values are the norm? What factors in the structure, daily patterns and values of schools impede the crucial and possible learning and growth I advocate?

In some ways this critique also applies to private schools and to elementary schools. But here I deal mainly with American public high schools, because that is where most of my experience as a teacher has been. And that is where American public education has been least open to the meaningful change it needs. In a 1978 workshop at the University of Maryland, the psychologist and educator William Glasser, author of *Schools Without Failure*[3], was asked why he had concentrated his work in elementary and junior high schools, rather than in high schools. His answer was that, as compared to the other school levels, high schools are a "tough nut to crack," and he did not want to get mired in that world. I doubt if Glasser's answer would be different today. My 30-year effort to crack that nut from the inside is the basis for this book.

The data

Throughout the book I quote some of the thoughts and ideas of former students to illustrate various points. These thoughts and ideas came from several sources and add a measure of reality to my analysis. They show that student perceptions of, and concerns and frustrations with, what constitutes good and bad teaching and learning, were about the same in 1991 as they were in 1964.

One source is 25 audio-taped conversations about schools and learning held with 79 students or former students in 1964, 1967, 1971, 1990 and 1991. Two sources of opinion come from written surveys: of 120 members of the Class of 1990, South Lakes High School, Reston, Virginia; and 102 South Lakes alums. I also used comments from various student course evaluations and letters, as well as letters from former students who wrote to share their experiences and their assessment of high school from the vantage point of one or more years out of school. The surveys were written by the students shortly before they graduated; they were asked not to put their names on the surveys. The student course evaluations were also anonymous. All former students' names used in the book have been changed unless written permission to use actual names has been received. Real names are indicated by the use of first and last names.[4]

How many people are actually fooled by the schools' games? I don't know. Probably many people are just weary of it all. They figure that somehow the schools *seem* to function and kids *seem* to learn something. So while many people have complaints and concerns, they don't have the energy, desire or will to understand, let alone to change, the schools. Well, I think schools can and must be better understood and changed. That's what this book is all about.

Notes

1. Thomas Hughes, Buccaneer Books reprint, 1987. This book has a vivid account of the physical abuse and awful conditions in a typical Public School in England in the early 19th century.
2. Grove Press, 1967
3. Harper & Row, 1969
4. In February 1990, I sent out questionnaires to 435 of my former students from the South Lakes classes of 1985 through 1989. Of these questionnaires, 102 were returned to me, completed, and 50 were returned, address unknown—a 25% return rate.

2

What Is Good Education?

At back-to-school night in the fall of each school year I always enjoyed the reaction of parents to the circle of chairs in my classroom. Of course, many kids had already told their parents about my keeping the students' chairs in a circle. Still, since most of the parents had a very different image of what a high school classroom is supposed to look like, they often were surprised or puzzled—and occasionally annoyed, asking "how can the kids learn in this kind of an arrangement?"

The circle is both a learning device and a metaphor for the essence of good education, the essence of genuine learning: students being actively involved with what they are learning. Active involvement assumes that teachers help students understand the purpose and value of what they are asked to learn. It assumes that teachers encourage students to challenge and engage the material presented, and encourages them to develop their own material, to seek their own resources—and to challenge that, also.

Genuine learning

I seek genuine learning—learning that *involves* students in the process, learning that students can see and hear and feel, learning that students can experience and not simply touch lightly. To have meaning for the learner, and not be something done mainly to fulfill an external demand (get a grade, please a parent, etc.), learning must be

- involving
- intellectually challenging
- exciting
- inviting
- nurturing
- non-confrontational

- self-directed and voluntary
- encouraging of personal growth and self-awareness

For good education to take place, the attributes listed above must be present. Kids should *want* to attend school, and should truly feel the school is theirs. Young people *do* want to learn, if only we let them. Can this kind of education be achieved? Of course it can.

Education should involve students in learning

Good education is an involving process in which people actively engage what they are learning. This can only happen in an interactive situation. The case for involvement—for active participation in learning— was put succinctly by a student on one of the June 1990 government course evaluations. Quoting an old proverb, this student wrote, in part: "When I hear, I forget. When I see, I remember. But when I do, I understand." Using the same proverb, another South Lakes student wrote on one of the senior surveys, in response to the question, "what were the best learning situations for you in high school?":

> Class discussions, teachers lecturing but involving the class or using creative approaches to keep class involved. Why? When I participate, I remember more. Phrase: "Tell me, I forget. Show me, I remember. Involve me, I understand." Very true!!

The interaction is not limited to a classroom of students sitting in a circle. It could take place in a science lab or a language lab or an art room or in a drama production or on a gym floor or a playing field. A student could interact with another student anywhere or interact, perhaps as an apprentice, with someone who is accomplishing a task or job that the student wants to learn about. It could occur on a field trip. It could happen in a library looking up information that leads students on to further information or insights that go beyond their starting point. It could be when writing an essay. Students could interact on a bus.

One of the most successful interactive learning situations I ever developed was on a school bus in the early 1960's at Northport High School, Long Island, New York. We were studying local issues in my government classes. I arranged for a school bus to be available for one class period at a time. It would drive to various neighborhoods or commercial areas of the school district. One or more students who lived in the destination area would have prepared a presentation about it, and would lead a discussion and answer other students' questions. Each class went on these one-period field trips several times. We did not spend much time off the bus, since we had only 40 minutes available to us. Most discussions took place on the bus. The discussions were incredible. Students who rarely said anything in class, who were academically unsuccessful in most school situations, raised good points and asked good questions. There was great interest in a variety of matters ranging from the spacing between houses to the effects on the community of a projected electric company power plant.

There was no magic at work here. Students were actively involved in planning the trips. Therefore, they were interested in the discussions. Moreover, the bus trip to different neighborhoods provided a laboratory for learning that allowed students to build on prior knowledge. This is an effective tool to increase the interest and understanding of the learner. To top off the experience, students wrote essays about the study of local issues that incorporated what they learned on the one-period bus trips.

A student can also interact with a book. I'm not being cute when I say "interact" with a book. There is a difference between decoding the words on a page and *reading* the book, thinking about what it says, even arguing with it—taking notes, making comments in the margin, underlining passages, and so forth. A former colleague, Nancy Nyrop, says she always reads with a pencil. I like that. She is involved with her reading. Students can be encouraged to do the same thing. This can happen when we see the purpose of education as developing adults who think and question, as opposed to training students to memorize isolated bits of information to be spit back on a test.

An emphasis on interaction and process does *not* mean that students learn no facts or information. The notion that facts and process are mutually incompatible is a false dichotomy. The question is not whether students learn facts but whether they learn them in a context that gives the facts meaning. Over and over again, students have told me that they are much more likely to truly learn *and understand* information if they acquire it experientially rather than abstractly, if they engage learning and don't simply absorb information which is easily forgotten later. Two former students supported this involvement theory in their alumni survey responses. Both of these students were academically successful students and quite capable of playing the game of school—doing well on tests, and performing well under any circumstances.

Tom, Class of 1989:

> Hands-on [experiences] always worked best for me. I remember going in to Washington with an art class to see the works that we had been studying about. I also remember the trip down to the Vir-

13

ginia Assembly [in Richmond] with our [government] class. Labs in chemistry and physics also reinforced the things we were being taught. Of course science projects were some of my greatest teachers. When I was challenged to figure out how to build and make something work, I couldn't just memorize a formula, I had to *know* the stuff. [Tom's emphasis]

Janice, Class of 1988:

The most valuable academic experiences I had in high school were those in which an open and frequent exchange between teacher and student was present. *A student must be actively involved on a day to day basis in his academic environment (homework not necessarily implied) in order to achieve and retain information covered in his classes.* [My emphasis]

Education should be intellectually challenging

Students should be immersed in ideas. They should be strongly encouraged to wrestle with those ideas, to explore them, to challenge them, to test them out in whatever ways are possible. Students can and should be taught to evaluate data and make discerning judgements about it. And they should be taught and encouraged to formulate opinions and test them out, too. Any academic class should do this. Unfortunately, this kind of stimulation is lacking in most public schools today.

For the most part, there is an the appearance of intellectual activity in the form of textbook assignments and frequent tests to "prove" students learned from the texts. Or, if students are assigned something more substantive, like a research paper, the central purpose of the assignment is very often buried under stylistic requirements of length, form, note cards, and draft copies of the paper. The central purpose of the assignment should be learning to do research and providing supporting evidence for questions the student has developed. The teacher should be helping the student learn ways to do the research, ways to develop the questions about their topics, ways to provide substantive evidence. Doing a research paper can be a daunting task for kids. It takes time and experience to become comfortable with developing a topic, with carrying out research, and with writing a paper that effectively documents the research and its results.

But what frequently happens with this kind of assignment is that teachers frighten kids into becoming more concerned about form than substance. They insist on only one way to do the task, only one way to research ideas or document data: one *must* use note cards, one *must* have

14

a draft copy, one *must* use only a certain form of documentation (endnotes instead of footnotes or, whatever the teacher tells the kids is orthodox). This is a negative approach that only undermines the intellectual value of the assignment and discourages many students from connecting with the substance of the task. And thus discouraged, they either do a sloppy job or don't do it at all. Naturally this drives most teachers crazy, and confirms in their minds that "these kids" are lazy, or "won't do what they are told." Most students are neither lazy nor stubborn; they often *are* unsure and overwhelmed.

Of course kids must learn about form and documentation of data; that is part of what a research paper is all about. But the operative word is *part*--not all. It is appropriate for teachers to suggest good ways to complete tasks; it is not appropriate to insist on one way and one way only. But students often report that teachers have told them just that. Nonsense. There are many ways to do research and document the data. The point is not *how* one documents data but that one *does* document data. Frequently, students say that if they stray from the exact way the teacher instructs, the paper is graded down or in some cases rejected. In fact much more weight may be given to these factors than to the paper's substance.

Or, teachers may grade a paper down if a draft copy or note cards have not been turned in. What is the assignment for? Is it to help the kids learn to develop a thesis, do research, document and write about it, or is the main purpose to show the kids who's boss?

Taking notes on note cards is a good idea. So is doing a draft copy of the paper. But if a student finds alternative ways to proceed, what difference does it make? Indeed, with an increasing number of kids having their own computers at home, it is more and more likely that kids will keep notes on their disks rather than on note cards. Can't you see the teacher going home at night with 135 kids' disks to check?

It is especially important when students are first learning ways to do research and document data that the focus be on substance and not form, on learning ways to develop topics, on ways to substantiate information, on developing and questioning ideas. Hook kids on research first; get them excited about exploring ideas and finding evidence. To get them started, let them work on some topic of interest to them. There is plenty of time later, once kids are hooked, to put more stress on form. To put unnecessary teacher requirements in the way of the real task destroys serious learning. It puts the cart before the horse. If form follows function in architecture, as Louis Sullivan said, it does in learning also.

Give assignments that force kids to reason. Don't just require them to memorize facts to be regurgitated on a test. Even students who usually are seen as poor academic students can rise to this challenge. Of course, one does not start out with highly abstract conceptual assignments. That kind of curve ball can only add to their discouragement. The degree of abstraction, or difficulty, of an assignment should depend in part on the teacher's assessment of the students' capacities at that point in their development to handle conceptual assignments.

Try something different

One semester at South Lakes High School I was asked to take a special group of 15 freshman and sophomore students who were failing their regular social studies classes (geography or world history) and who, according to their teachers, were likely to fail the year.[1] These were students with altogether poor academic records, and, not surprisingly, students with generally low self-esteem (especially when it came to school work). To begin, I asked them to tell about one thing they had learned from their first semester social studies class. Not *one* of the students could recall anything.

These kids were frustrated about school, angry about being "failures." This was disguised behind bravado and disruptive behavior. So I gave them an assignment that made sense to them: make a map of the route from your house to the school. The map had to include landmarks, street names, and be as proportionately accurate as possible. Sounds simple, eh? Not so.

Many of these students simply could not conceptualize a map. Some had no idea what the route was, since they used a school bus and never watched its route. The only way some of these students could begin to grasp the assignment was to walk a bit from the school and from their houses to get a sense of the street patterns. After much effort all 15 did complete a map. Not all the maps were of equal clarity or accuracy, but they were all reasonably clear and accurate. And the assignment provided a basis to launch into a deeper study of the geography and history of Reston and Northern Virginia. For example, by studying their maps, the students began to see relationships between the way Reston (a planned new town) is designed and the location of different types of housing, open spaces and shopping centers. This even led to a short study of the socio-economic make-up of Reston.

By itself, the map assignment did not convert these students into scholars for whom abstract, conceptual thinking is second nature. But it *did* open the door to their beginning to reason and conceptualize. Near the end of the semester, I conducted a group evaluation in the circle. The students felt good about their academic improvement. Without warning, I asked them to list on a sheet of paper everything they had learned in the class. They all made relevant comments about what they learned and how they liked the class. Then we talked about what they wrote, in contrast to what they were unable to do at the beginning of the semester. All but one of the 15 passed the course that semester; the one who failed stopped coming to the course altogether, unfortunately.

I very clearly remember the comment made to me one day just before class began by Darryl, a freshman who had been failing most of his other courses that year. Quite out of the blue, about half-way through the semester, he said to me, "Hey, man, I think I can think, can't I?" And when I replied, "Of course you can, Darryl," he said, "It's ok!" As he flashed a big smile at me, I realized he felt it was ok for him to admit he could think. This was a student for whom school was an almost constant series of frustrations. He seldom smiled at teachers. My pleasure at his comment was great, to say the least!

Kids have a difficult time grasping the concept of redistricting, or gerrymandering, of election districts. So early in my teaching career I devised an assignment that required students to learn about gerrymandering by doing some inductive reasoning.

The kids were given two maps of San Francisco and some socio-economic data about areas in the city. Prior to the assignment the students had learned about which groups of people the Democratic and Republican parties have generally attracted in the last 50 years or so. The students had also learned that the party in control of the state legislature at the time of redistricting (after the decennial census mandated by the U.S. Constitution) usually tries to draw election districts in such a way as to benefit itself. This is often hard for kids to understand.

The first map showed the shape of the city's two congressional districts in 1941, after the Democratic Party, which then controlled the California legislature, had drawn congressional districts based on the 1940 census to benefit itself. The second map was blank. So, using the information about political parties and the socio-economic data about various parts of San Francisco, the assignment was to draw the congressional districts to show how the Republican Party might re-draw the districts to benefit itself after it gained control of the Legislature in the 1950 election.

The assignment was successful in helping the students use their reasoning powers to learn both facts and concepts. It should not have been difficult (indeed, a more sophisticated version of the assignment would have required kids to find their own data about the city). But because assignments like this *are* more intellectually challenging than, and quite different from, the typical kind of assignment, it takes students time to take advantage of them. Students are used to the more common didactic instruction—lecture or a textbook chapter with homework questions and/or a test on the lecture or chapter. The textbook may even include a diagram of a gerrymandering situation, but that is not the same as asking students to draw their own election districts. In fact, some kids resist doing this kind of task because it *is* more difficult than a straight textbook assignment. Other kids may initially think the assignment is silly or easy since it does not require the usual kind of homework. Of course, many kids are bored with typical homework. They expect to be bored but assume that the time-consuming nature of the typical homework is "hard work," and thus the truly hard work of trying to interpret data and draw an election district map based on it is too easy! Many kids have actually told me this.

But in time most students do learn to appreciate intellectually challenging assignments. One student put it like this on one of the 1990 government course evaluations:

> I think I have learned much of value this year. This course was different than most of my other courses. We didn't have tests every week and a page of homework in a textbook every night. Some people might think that the course was easier than most because there wasn't as much "busywork" as in other courses. However, I don't think this is true. In many ways, this course was more challenging than most because you *had* to think. In most cases it's possible to get a good grade without thinking or learning much of anything. This isn't the case in government [class].

Should learning be passive?

Most school learning still is passive. Students do not interact with what they learn. They are expected to absorb information and then heave it back on a test.

There are valid uses for memorization as a part of the learning process. For example, one must learn the multiplication tables to master arithmetic. There may be value in memorizing spelling words if we continue to use the words in later writing. It is useful to memorize the locations of countries on maps. Yet even in these kinds of exercises it is vital that students understand why they must memorize the tables or words. The reason this kind of information is memorable is because adults continue to use it in their daily lives. And as they use it the purpose and value of what was memorized becomes clearer.

However, memorizing facts should not be the main diet for students. What is the value of memorizing historical dates or information when one could be learning the sweep of the past, the various historians' concepts and interpretations of the past, and its relevance for today? In that context learning dates and facts are more meaningful and easier. Why memorize the 18 powers of Congress in Article I, Section 8 of the Constitution, when one could be learning the general functioning and purposes of Congress and the issues it confronts, and through that process learning its 18 powers? What is the value of memorizing grammar rules without understanding written and oral language use? Why memorize scientific formulas or data unless one uses this information in a lab and sees its purpose?

Ask most students what they remember after taking a test on memorized material. Not much. George, a 1989 South Lakes graduate, wrote on his alumni survey that the worst kind of learning situations were:

> The kind where you were expected to know the material taught until 5 minutes after you were tested on it and then send it to some dank, forgotten skid row in the never-never land of your brain (most of high school was like this).

So what has been achieved by forcing students to memorize to pass a test? Very little beyond maybe increasing test scores and creating the illusion that the students have learned something. If our goal is to produce students who can excel at Trivial Pursuit®[2], then *perhaps* this kind of passive learning is what we want. But it is not what we *should* want.

Thinking can be risky

Students can find it risky to become immersed in an intellectually challenging discussion. Young people are afraid of being seen as wrong. Often they are hesitant to give an answer that might be wrong, or express ideas with which, they think, most other students (or the teacher) may disagree. This kind of fear may or may not be natural. But school experiences that condition kids to rote learning exacerbate it. Supplying pat answers rather than learning to interpret data, to think and to test out ideas enhances that fear. Kids need to grapple intellectually with each other as well as with the teacher, and to learn that frequently there are *no* pat answers.

Teachers *do* need to help students in this task. They need continually to help kids see the connections among facts and their relationship to concepts. When a teacher creates an environment in which kids feel able to risk suggesting interpretations of data and offering opinions, kids themselves soon learn to make connections among factors, to think conceptually and to learn to *reason*, both deductively and inductively. Without this kind of environment, students tend to turn off serious intellectual pursuits.

Killing curiosity

Additionally, kids need the chance to make mistakes, yes, to fail, and discover it is ok: one can learn that way too. Alas, there is much evidence that schools frequently kill or seriously wound kids' natural curiosity to learn. These comments are from audio-taped conversations with South Lakes graduates in May and July 1990:

Jason Kosnoski, class of 1988, talks about the role of the teacher:

> . . . the teacher has a very special role in presenting things to the students . . . it's not like the teacher comes into the school and says, "hey, what are we going to do, guys" you know, and then you have some sort of decision . . . by consensus. But the teacher *can* present certain facts and run it by the class, and the teacher . . . is . . . in that unique position of having the knowledge, but whether they are dictatorial or whether they are semi-democratic is totally up to the teacher.

Peter, class of 1990, talks about the value of making mistakes and learning from them during an independently-planned trip to the Supreme Court with two other students:

Peter: Let me break in with another positive thing that I just thought of. This hands-on experience for me . . . like in . . . government [class], you know . . . going to the Supreme Court was a terrible experience in a way because we had no idea what we were doing, but therefore when I came back, through doing that I learned that I would do it better next time, and I did see [that the experience] . . . let me screw up, basically, and I will know [next time] . . . you know what I'm saying?

Tripp: That's right. I don't know of a better way on this earth to learn anything . . .

Peter: . . . than to screw up . . .

Tripp: That's right! As long as you know that . . . your life isn't on the line . . . you can afford to do that, right?

Peter: Right!

Emily and Manny, class of 1990, and Elsie, Class of 1989, talk about the matter of schools stifling kids' curiosity during an audio-taped conversation in May 1990:

Emily: I have a five year old little brother and I was noticing how he is always so inquisitive and always wants to know everything and he's always asking questions, he like really has a strong desire to learn and I'm wondering if maybe when we all were younger and started to go to school, and you get a bad grade in math and you think, that's it, I'm bad in math for the rest of my life. My sister gets straight A's but she got a bad grade in handwriting and she still writes like a slob because she doesn't think she can do any better. Maybe it just discouraged her.

Manny: They [schools] don't encourage the curiosity people start out with.

Elsie: I think it's like so true because . . . I think people naturally have this innate curiosity to learn about things you don't know, but when you get a system and you get monotony, you get broken down, and it becomes, "I don't want to do this." And [schools] have to make sure that every single person has to have the same X, Y, Z education and when you look at it . . . it's the death of curiosity.

In fact, public schools not only wound if not kill curiosity, they are a hotbed of anti-intellectualism. There are several reasons for this.

One is that, sad to say, far too many teachers tend to be anti-intellectual. Responding to intellectual curiosity requires energy and a willingness to cope with the unexpected. New ideas do not follow previously established patterns; nor do old ideas which are new to the students. A teacher whose way of teaching is to routinely adhere to rigid patterns is not likely either to encourage or respond well to intellectual curiosity. Unfortunately, a large segment of teachers teach this way.

The anti-intellectualism of all too many teachers is reinforced by the system. It rewards teachers who play it safe, who don't rock the boat, who don't get into trouble with parents. It goes so far as to promote safe teachers to be administrators! Teachers who play it safe, who go by the book (literally, teaching mainly or only from the textbook), are much less likely to encourage or support intellectual curiosity.

Evaluating progress can be negative, too

The evaluation (grading) patterns used by most school systems also reinforce anti-intellectualism. These generally require teachers to reduce the assessment of students to letter or number grades. Moreover, there is strong pressure on teachers to give students frequent grades: one or two quizzes a week, very short superficial writing assignments (if any at all), and the like.

Although one *can* limit the negative effect of assessment devices, not many teachers do. One consequence of adhering to a rigid grading system is that teachers tend to give assignments that can be easily graded by a letter or number. The frequent assessment of small pieces of work (quizzes, short writing samples) reduces kids' opportunities to try things out and to grapple with new ways of learning because they are being judged every step of the way. Thus, many teachers shy away from assigning essays or other projects that require grappling with complex matters that do not lend themselves to quick, pat answers. Creative, thoughtful teachers certainly *do* give these creative assignments, and manipulate the letter/number grading system to intelligently evaluate them. Regrettably, such teachers are in a minority. Most teachers accept the system's grading requirements. And, the system of letter or number grades has been with us for so long that most students and parents assume and expect evaluation by them. The end result is to ensure that students will have a fact-gathering experience that can be awarded a clear-cut grade rather than have an intellectually challenging experience.

For most students, then, serious intellectual pursuit is something they see the "smart kids" do. This, too, is reinforced by the system. Tracking, the system of creating separate classes for so-called academically brighter and poorer students, creates the notion that some kids can think creatively while others can only learn by rote. Well, it just isn't so. Virtually any student can do intellectually challenging work, can be taught and encouraged to reason and question and make discerning judgements. Not all students are able to handle the same level of abstraction, or can develop a high level of intellectual pursuit. But it is possible to build on the natural curiosity of virtually all kids and to teach them to develop their capacities for intellectual rigor.

The prevalence of rote-learning is reflected in the general anti-intellectualism of our society. As a whole, American culture hardly even pays lip-service to the value of intellectual pursuit. And we don't do any better in public schools. And where, if not in school, should intellectual pursuit flourish? Schools go out of their way to honor athletes, with pep rallies several times during the school year, and rituals such as "spirit week," designed to increase rah-rah related to a sports event and to drum up something called school spirit all year long. There also are frequent announcements on the public address system reminding the students of up-coming sports events and encouraging attendance at them. And of course there is major media coverage of high school (as well as college and professional) athletics and athletes.

Of course athletes should be given due recognition. Of course athletics should be covered by the media. But the line between due recognition and glorification is a thin one. And this attention to, and often glorification of, athletes and athletics reflects part of our value system. Where is the similar level of attention to, and glorification of, intellectual pursuit? Shouldn't that, too, be part of our value system?

How often do schools have pep rallies honoring academic achievement or encouraging mental activities? The possibilities boggle the mind. Can't you see the cheer leaders encouraging students gathered in the gym or auditorium to chant:

Rah, rah, hip hooray; Alfred Garcia got an A!

In fact, high schools *do* sometimes have assemblies honoring academics. And most high school graduation ceremonies still maintain the custom of having the class valedictorian give a speech. During the school year there may be announcements on the public address system about this or that student who won an academic distinction, just as the media do announce Nobel prizes.

But such honoring of academic achievement is cursory and infrequent. We have not made intellectual pursuit a high value in our culture. It doesn't grab us. It doesn't grab students because students need rewards. But schools fail to show them that intellectual pursuit *is* rewarding and even fun. The playground of the mind is different from that of the body, but good exercise and fun in its own way. Leading students to this discovery should be a primary goal of all schools.

Education should be exciting

Students should be excited about learning. That's not asking too much. As it is now in most high schools, they aren't. Being excited about learning does not mean students will constantly jump for joy. It does mean they will feel compelled to seek out knowledge, to discover new ideas, to gain new insights. They will be compelled by their own curiosity and rewarded by their new understanding. Moreover, being excited about education means students will actually carry ideas and knowledge generated in school beyond school, to home and friends. Students will see such ideas and knowledge as a real part of their lives, not something to be left at the schoolhouse door.

High school kids do not often share what is going on in class with parents and friends. When they leave a classroom they generally put what happened there in the farthest recesses of their minds until they have to do something about it (such as homework). When kids leave a classroom talking animatedly about what just went on, something is different. When they tell you that last night they talked at home about things discussed in class, something is happening. When they start applying information learned in class to the rest of their life, and see that it is important to do this, you know you have struck pay dirt. This kind of thing is rare—in

23

great part because of the way schools now operate—but it *does* happen. However, as I keep saying over and over, it takes the right environment to make it happen. Part of that environment is to get kids to see that the learning really is for *them*, not for a grade, not to please someone else. As I used to say to kids all the time, "you have to buy into your own education." Here is an interesting observation about these issues from a 1990 government course evaluation:

> This year the single most important thing I've learned is that one must buy into their education in order to get anything out of it. I have found from the IIPS projects [year-long group projects] at the end of the year that because I was interested in these subjects and therefore listened, I paid attention and learned! At night I go home and discuss bonds, the federal deficit, the environment, and important issues such as AIDS, welfare and the homeless. The best feeling is that I got as much out of this and it was all for my own benefit, not a grade! I love it!! It makes me feel good that I can learn because at this point of senior slump most of my other classes are having no effect on my brain except to scare me into thinking it will continue in college next year.

Education should be inviting, nurturing, and non-confrontational

In a talk given to Fairfax County, Virginia, educators in the mid-1970's, William Purkey, author of *Self-Concept and School Achievement*[3] observed that too often schools *dis*-invite kids to school, rather than invite them. Yes, indeed. He meant that the cumulative effect of many of the rules and practices of schools results in an unstated but very clear message to the kids: behave exactly as we say or we don't want you.

Dan, a 1988 South Lakes graduate, wrote in his alumni survey response about feeling welcome:

> I think that teachers should become more involved with the individual student . . . I believe that teachers should stress asking students to speak to them after school. If my teacher made me feel welcome after school I . . . enjoyed the class more.

All kids should feel welcome during and after school, should feel they belong and that the adults who run the show, the teachers and administrators and counselors and librarians and custodians and secretaries, truly want the kids there. This may seem obvious, but the message that many kids get is that they are not welcome. This is especially so for students who do not easily fit into the academic or behavioral expectations of the school, the so-called slow or nonacademic students—those who frequently run afoul of the school's rules. Even when it's difficult for teachers and others to work with kids who do not fit neatly into the niches provided by the system, public schools really *are* for everyone.

A few years ago Ken Plum addressed this fact very effectively when he spoke to several government class at South Lakes High about the way the Virginia General Assembly functions. Plum is the Director of Adult Education for the Fairfax County Public Schools and a delegate to the Assembly. When I commented between classes that the next group of kids wasn't likely to ask as sharp questions, Plum replied: "The parents send us the best they have and we have to take them all." Indeed.

We/they or we/we?

Schools generally tend to exhibit a we/they mentality, with "we," the adults who are in charge opposed to "they," the students.

Instead, teachers and administrators should ask kids to join with them in an inviting, nurturing, non-confrontational educational environment where "we," the adults work with "we," the students. The adults who teach and train and supervise kids should see themselves on the same side as the kids, not as their adversaries. As George, quoted earlier, put it on his alumni survey:

> High school would be much better suited to educating people if the attitudes of students and teachers towards one another could be improved. Unfortunately . . . the resentment both parties feel towards one another will probably continue. If there is a solution to these problems, it lies not with more disciplining of the students, but in more understanding between student and teacher.

A confrontational, adversarial environment does not nurture kids' natural curiosity, or nurture in them a love of learning, a love of intellectual pursuit. Moreover, a we/we educational environment does not mean that the teacher is not in charge. Of course the teacher is in charge. Even the most independent, mature high school seniors want the help and guidance of teachers. But students want this in a way that shows respect for them, that treats them with dignity, that assumes they have brains and feelings, that assumes they know things and have insights they can share with others, including the teacher. In short, kids want the same treatment as the rest of us do—the golden rule applies here, too.

Maintaining serious intellectual rigor and developing students' abilities to reason and make intelligent judgements are far more likely in a we/we environment than in a we/they environment. Here is what Kate

Sproul, another 1989 South Lakes graduate, said about this on her alumni survey:

> The best learning situations for me were debates where everyone listened to each other and didn't interrupt, and discussions in which students were able to interact with the teacher and the class and express their own opinions. These ways of teaching helped me learn *because I had to know enough to be able to state, support, and defend my own opinion.* [my emphasis] I also had to be open-minded enough to listen to other people and accept some part of their ideas or refute their ideas. Either way I had to explain why.

As a general rule, the best that can be hoped for in a we/they situation is that students will come away not too badly scathed, and will have acquired some information and skills that they may be able to develop and make use of in their later lives.

One of the characteristics of a dis-inviting, non-nurturing, confrontational environment is that it is also highly competitive. Students are encouraged to see each other, as well as teachers, as adversaries. This may not be the result of a conscious, deliberate effort, but it is a common consequence of an environment in which teachers judge kids competitively and frequently compare them to one another. Like so many characteristics of public schools, this competitive factor is also a reflection of values and practices in the society at large. An interesting comment on competition and schools was made by Karl, a Yellow Springs, Ohio, high school student, in an audio-taped conversation in June 1971, a few days before he graduated:

> One thing that's always bugged me about school is it's been a very competitive atmosphere, and I don't think learning should be competitive. I think there's a natural competition between people, but there's also a lot of things in school that make it a lot more competitive than it should be. And that's always bugged me. I draw a line between competition out on a tennis court and the competition in learning. Because different people are going to learn different ways.

Competitiveness may be natural, as Karl said, though I have my doubts. But if it is, surely it is greatly and unnecessarily exacerbated in public schools. A competitive milieu is counterproductive to serious learning. Competition tends to reduce the focus from substantive learning to a game quality, where the aim is to win, not learn. On the one hand, there is much rhetoric in the school world about "individualizing" learning—that is, recognizing that students learn differently and have different needs. On the other hand, the competitive factor tends to undercut the benefits of individualizing.

There are many ways to create an inviting, nurturing, non-confrontational environment, of course. Not all teachers need to work with kids the same way. Kids can respond to a variety of approaches. There are successful teachers who regularly give tests and quizzes with few if any doubts about them and who accept without much question the letter/number grading system. Most kids can learn from both creative teachers and the more tedious norm. Sally, a student at South Lakes discussed the differences in teachers. She said that enthusiastic teachers make the classroom interesting. When teachers show that they care about the kids, and really do help them, "We want to come to [their] classes," she said.

There are two vital characteristics required of an inviting educational environment: students must feel cared about and must be able to get real help.

As one student put it on the 1990 government course evaluation:

> Come now, Mr. Tripp, what have we learned? Ask me to write *another* [student's emphasis] 10 page essay! Yes, very much so the atmosphere of the class has a major influence on my learning. Treat people like adults and that is how they will act, at least mostly.

Education should be self-directed and voluntary

It is imperative that teachers and administrators—and students and parents—understand how crucial self-direction is. Serious learning takes place only when the learner wants to learn, when the learner sees the value and purpose of learning something, when the learner is curious and excited about learning something and when the learner is essentially in charge of his or her own learning. Learning must involve the heart as well as the mind. Students must buy into their own learning. They must value it. They must learn primarily for learning's sake, because they see it as having to do with themselves. Adolescents can and do understand the need to become serious, productive, aware people. They all understand this in different ways, but for all kids it is a part of their natural curiosity about the world and how they fit into it.

Self-direction must be developed and nurtured. That is one function school *could* serve. One student on the 1990 government course evaluation put it like this: "Having a teacher to guide the way is very important, but with you learning is still self-directed."

Or, school can kill this natural curiosity and produce students who learn for external reasons (to get a grade, etc.). Not much learning that is done primarily to satisfy external demands sticks. More important, if such learning sticks it generally does so mainly to make it possible to spout isolated, unrelated facts or because it is reinforced with later experiences. For learning to have meaning, it must help students not only develop their intellectual capacities to the fullest possible extent, but help them become aware, critical, involved people. This can only happen when learning is essentially self-directed and voluntary.

People must understand that the appearance of learning found generally in public schools is, in the truest and fullest sense, not learning. Here is what Jason, quoted earlier, said about school learning in general:

> . . . so much of school is always the same, you go in and take tests. But you don't get a chance to make your own [mind up] . . . to express your own thoughts and have that be part of the curriculum because the curriculum was usually so rigid.

And this is how Tom, also quoted above, talked about school learning on his alumni survey:

> The least valuable [experiences in high school] were the daily grind and b.s. So many days I came home thinking: I spent six hours in school, and could have gotten all the stuff we did done in an hour. Half of our days were spent taking attendance, listening to substitutes, etc . . . In terms of academic stuff: straight memorization, lectures without any discussion. These are two that come to mind. They both give knowledge, but without *thought*. [Tom's emphasis] Again to learn something and have it stay with you, you need to think about it.

What these and most students cry out for is a chance to *really* learn, to think, to get involved, to direct their own destinies.

This relates to many of the issues analyzed in this book: the conflicting perceptions of the purpose of education; the whole idea of how and for what purpose we test students; the behavior of teachers and administrators; the structure of the schools; patterns of teaching and learning; the conditioning of students, and the place of young people in our culture and how they are dealt with. Self-direction, then, is central to genuine education and learning. It is a theme throughout this book.

Education must encourage personal growth and self-awareness

"All serious work in fiction is autobiographical," wrote the novelist Thomas Wolfe in his preface to *Look Homeward, Angel*[4]. All serious learning is autobiographical too, in that anything important becomes a part of ourselves. Moreover, we see and hear the world through the prism of our own experiences and personalities. In a very real sense, we learn through ourselves: we filter in and out of our consciousness the facts and ideas and insights we acquire, whether in school or anywhere else. Therefore, for education to have meaning, for us to make intelligent use of what we learn, we must understand ourselves. Understanding ourselves—becoming self-aware—means that we must understand our own feelings and perceptions and our own values. Thus, education must help students grow personally as well as intellectually. It must help them become as self-aware as possible.

Of course, not all of education should become a therapy session. But it is important for teachers to encourage students to become self-aware by creating a learning environment in which they can grow personally. It is axiomatic how much more one understands about information one takes in, as well as about one's beliefs, ideas and of course feelings, if one is self-aware. Phyllis, a 1987 South Lakes graduate, put it like this on her alumni survey response:

> . . . I learned best whenever I felt a personal revelation about the material, or whenever I made a "personal" contact with it . . . special teachers [who] stand out [do so] because in their classes I had a personal and intimate encounter with the subject they taught. Or, in other words, they did something special to "introduce me" to their specialty. If they didn't introduce me to the subject, me, Phyllis, then it probably had very little effect on me.

Students understand the relationship between learning and the self. The comments of two former students on their 1990 government course evaluations testify to this:

> From . . . other activities that we have done this year I have learned about myself. I've grown up mentally —that's what I am pleased about. I'm happy that I can have an intelligent conversation . . . knowing what I am talking about. Also the activities made me more aware of issues that have been important in the U.S. and around the world. Thanks, Mr. Tripp, for making me a part of the polity because now I actually feel a part of it, and I'm glad.

> I have learned from this class the basics of government but more

importantly I have learned from you how to sort out my ideas and where my values and responsibilities lie, which after all is going to be more useful in life as well as in my dealings with the government in my future. Thanks. A loving student.

Of course, it isn't only students who should be self-aware and grow personally. As Arthur Jersild noted long ago[5], self-awareness is at least as important for teachers and administrators in order for them to work effectively with kids. Unfortunately, far too many have little self-awareness. They frequently misunderstand the behavior of kids. They take personally things they should not. They rarely enjoy as people the students they teach and are constantly in an adversarial relationship with them. Such teacher behavior impedes serious learning, and stifles students' own growth and enjoyment.

In conclusion

This chapter is concluded with comments from several former students on their perceptions of good education. The comments cover the span from 1967 to 1990. The earlier conversations, reflecting the late 60's and early 70's, not surprisingly have something of a ring of free choice. In the later comments the emphasis tends to be more on applying learning to one's own experience. But these are minor differences of emphasis. The common thread among all the comments from the 60's to the 90's is that students want honesty, genuine help, and a chance to learn for themselves, to test out the world on their own terms.

First is an excerpt from an audio-taped conversation among three Northport High School seniors in May 1967. This dialogue focused on how honest the kids thought their dealings with teachers had been and on how much adult guidance they thought they needed.

Kristal: Well, as far as my education goes, I'd say that certain teachers are honest.

Aaron: Talking about this honesty thing, I think it's hard for the student to be honest with the teacher because the student has to get good marks, and that's important, so he's going to cheat and try to do other things to get the [grade]. It's important for the kid . . . You need to be guided.

Kristal: No! You don't have to be guided. Well, yes, you have to be pointed in a direction to see.

Aaron: There's a line between pointing and pushing. I mean how do you know when one teacher's pointing or pushing?

Delbert: There is a great deal of inhibition involved with education. Teachers often try to intimidate students in a line, which I don't think is right because they say, well look at Johnny Jones, class genius, don't you want to be like him? And certain people just don't.

Kristal: That's right. The whole thing I think is wrong with the school system is they make kids think they have to be a certain kind. They don't let kids recognize their own abilities for themselves. The fact [is] that we need janitors and cleaning women, and we also need lawyers and doctors . . . you need every kind of person.

Delbert: I want . . . to ask Aaron a question about why do you feel that you have to be guided?

Aaron: I'm not that mature, I'm not that . . . someone's gotta tell . . .

Kristal: Well, I don't think maturity comes from being guided, pulled by the nose . . . I don't think that's really learning. That's part of education too—learning to accept your own responsibility.

Aaron: But I know somebody's gotta set an example to look at.

Kristal: Well, I'm sure after you get out of school there's not going to be anyone there standing at your back every minute.

Aaron: No, but look. Say in education, there's a terrific difference between having a teacher drag you around by the nose and having him give you a direction to look in. You don't have to take that direction. I think if he shows you a direction I think that's the way a teacher should look at it, not as if he should guide a person down a straight and narrow [path].

Next is an excerpt of an audio-taped conversation among several Yellow Springs High School seniors in June 1971, in response to the question, "What should a high school education be?" Without hesitation, these were the responses:

Sally: It should be helping you grow up. A lot of people are just going to be put out into everyday life, that's where they end up going, and they won't be able to handle it. Like I think the New York trip is very helpful in that way. [Refers to a 5-day class trip to New York City.] Now, New York always in my mind was a bad place, you couldn't even walk on the streets in the day, and now I have a completely different look. I'm not scared of it at all, and I want to go back and everything like that. I think that's the sort of thing, it should be more of a look at the world instead of wasting all that time cramming all that information down your throat.

Norm: I forgot to bring that up on the first question, but the New York trip really taught me a lot about survival.

Gert: I sort of agree with Sally in that it should just help you to deal with yourself and accept yourself as important, and accept other people. And I guess it sounds just like Mr. Tripp but I think he's right, to get tools to learn by because you're not always going to be going to a class and having assignments and tests and everything, just help you to learn, or help you to find out the best way you can learn.

Chuck: While I was in junior high, I always thought up to eighth grade they were teaching you the skill; and I always thought high school was for the learning how to use the skills. But then we got to high school and they kept doing the same thing . . . but in social studies when we discuss something you just don't discuss the information, you discuss how it relates to everything in the world and how you can use it. Like it's also sort of made my mind so searching, like when I read books I'm more thinking about what I read.

Mort: They don't teach you how to apply your knowledge. And like I've seen a lot of people, they know a lot of things about certain categories but they don't know really how to apply their knowledge.

In another audio-taped conversation between two other Yellow Springs High Seniors in June 1971, Karl, quoted earlier, and Mel discussed their desire that high school education focus on enhancing the choices students have:

Mel: I think a high school is to open choice [to students] I don't think a high school student is too young to be able to stand out on his own as to what he thinks he might be interested in. And I think there's a lot of pressure on the high school student that you have to take these courses because they are going to be required of you in college. And I think there's a lot of pressure on the idea of getting things done on time, taking these certain steps, getting ready for college, and I think that's a lot of crap. I think it would be much better if a person could experiment on his own as to what he is interested in.

Karl: I think that the first 2 years of high school should be set up so that you have a course that touched on a variety of things and a wide variety. And in your last 2 years you should be able to choose what courses you want and pursue those . . . I think the biggest thing that I would like to see in my high school education is learning to deal with people and society. Sitting in a classroom doesn't give you that. So I think that the high school would probably have to change and offer some sort of . . . courses where you study people and that sort of thing. I think that would be very helpful, especially with those who aren't going on to college.

Finally, Kate Sproul, also quoted above (again from her alumni survey response) on the relationship between the way students are treated, the value of the education, and playing the game of school:

One thing that struck me senior year was that all of my teachers treated us as adults and respected us as such. In the other three years,

32

the teachers considered us to be children. In both cases, we lived up to the teachers' expectations of us. Class discussions in which we were encouraged to express our opinions were greatly appreciated because we were treated as equals with valid ideas instead of as little kids. I realize that a lot of maturing occurs between freshman and senior year and that it is foolish to give freshman as much freedom as seniors, but they can handle a lot more freedom and responsibility than they usually get. Some teachers are so afraid of losing control of their classes they completely stifle everyone's curiosity and let the class know that their opinions aren't welcomed. The teacher doesn't respect the class, so the class retaliates by misbehaving, and the teacher helps along what he/she was trying to prevent. Some teachers only want the students to regurgitate the teacher's ideas. Nothing is learned from this kind of teaching.

I spent ¾ of my senior year writing what I thought. The last quarter I wrote what my English teacher wanted to read because it was the only way to save my grade. Many teachers give you a tough choice: express your own opinions and be your own person or get a decent grade. Students that are going on to college have to get good grades. Students who show their parents their report cards have to get good grades. We learn when we first start school to focus on grades and forget about how much we learn.

Notes

1. The fact that this was a class of only 15 kids is significant, of course. But while the relatively small class size was a factor in how I handled the class, nothing that I did with those kids could not be done with similar students in the more typical larger-sized class of 25 or 30.
2. A trademark of Horn Abbot Ltd., distributed and sold in the U.S. by Parker Brothers, a Division of Tonka Corp., Beverly, MA 01915
3. Prentice-Hall, 1970
4. Charles Scribner's Sons, 1929, p.xvii
5. *When Teachers Face Themselves*, Teachers College, Columbia, 1955

3

Circles in Square Rooms

Sitting in a circle can be scary. There is no place to hide. It is easy to feel vulnerable. But sitting in a circle of chairs in a classroom can also be enjoyable—and can open the door to a level of involvement in learning that is not possible in a conventional arrangement of chairs and desks in rows.

The circle is not a gimmick. Of all the learning techniques that promote good education, that provide serious opportunities for students to learn and grow, none is more important than the circle.

For many students, sitting in a classroom with the chairs arranged in a circle *is*, at first, scary and unsettling. Most of them get used to it. A few resist to the end of the school year. But there is no doubt that in a circle arrangement most students become more actively involved in the work of the course than happens when they sit in rows.

Necessity being the mother of invention, it was desperation that caused me to move from the conventional rows to the circle in the fall of 1964. The students were becoming restless, and were getting less and less involved in the work of the course. Learning seemed to be at a minimum. There were far too many personal side conversations among the students during class. Most of them were good academic students and all were very nice kids. But the classes were not clicking. One day it dawned on me that interaction among the students about class topics would be much more likely if people faced each other. So I decided to try a circle.

When students came in the room their comments ran the gamut from "Hey, this is neat" to "What's going on here?" to "This is stupid." But soon they settled down. As I took my seat in the circle, I explained my reasons for the new arrangement. I wanted to encourage open, honest dialogue among all the class members. By having people face each other, I hoped they would become more involved. I hoped that side conversations during general class discussions would be less tempting. Just maybe they would feel less bored. If so, they would learn more. I wanted the students to know that this arrangement would make it easier to learn from each other and not only from me.

Within a week, the classes came alive. There was less boredom and more involvement; there were fewer side conversations. During the balance of the 1964–65 school year we used the circle arrangement, though from time to time we did return to rows of desks. This provided some variety and helped me test out the circle's value more fully. The students' behavior was closely tied to room arrangement. Most students *were* more involved in class discussions when seated in a circle.

More than a technicality

Classroom arrangement is not a mere technicality, or simply a part of the teacher's style. It reflects assumptions about the teaching-learning process and its outcome. The usual classroom seating arrangement of rows headed by the teacher at the front assumes that virtually all information comes from the teacher; it assumes a teacher-centered, teacher-dominated classroom in which the teaching/learning process depends upon the teacher lecturing, or asking students questions about an assignment to reinforce facts, with students absorbing the information and periodically spitting it back on an exam. It assumes that dialogue about the class subject is directed solely to and from the teacher, not among the students.

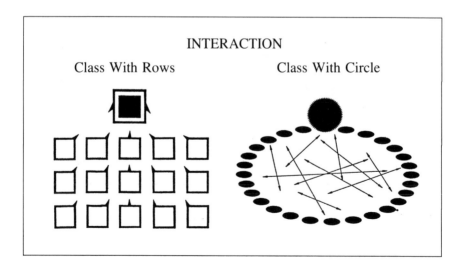

INTERACTION

Class With Rows   Class With Circle

But it is precisely the set of assumptions reflected in the typical classroom arrangement of chairs in rows that is at the heart of what is wrong with high school education. In general, students *are* bored, and study (if they do at all) mainly to get grades, not to learn concepts or ideas or even facts for their own value. And this is the case largely because students are not involved in their own learning.

But people learn from their own experiences as well as from reading. They also learn from sharing ideas and experiences with each other. Putting student chairs in a circle certainly does not guarantee that the students will be more involved, but it does make it much more likely. Here is how two students put it on their 1990 government course evaluations:

> I've learned more about how our government works, and the relationship between our government and its citizens. Within the circle students can see other students and discussion becomes more involved with several opinions . . . Hearing what other people have to say plays a big part in what I think, how strong or weak I fight for my beliefs and right to an opinion.

> I learned this year from the unique way you've set up this room. It really makes a difference when we are all facing each other. This promotes learning in my opinion.

If the circle arrangement is so good, why isn't it more common? There are a couple of reasons. One is that most teachers think it is easier for them to maintain control while standing up in front of a class arranged in rows. And for most teachers, control is very important. Actually, however, control is easier in the circle: the teacher can more readily see all the students and it is harder for them to hide. A second reason that teachers shun the circle is that many of them are not comfortable entering into freewheeling discussions with students. Most teachers want certainty, and in open-ended discussions that engage students in exploring issues there seldom is certainty. Indeed, until they get used to it, some students also are uncomfortable in this kind of atmosphere. But it is the teacher who sets the tone for the class, so if the teacher is comfortable, kids soon learn to be. One gets an idea of how unusual the circle is from this comment by another student on one of the 1990 government class evaluations:

> This class is good. I learned lots. The circle of chairs is infinitely superior to desks in neat, uniform rows. [They] are a breath of fresh air . . . I'm certainly enlightened.

Rows work sometimes, too

Of course there are learning situations, such as a formal lecture, where the usual classroom seating arrangement is valid, perhaps even necessary. This arrangement does not necessarily mean that kids will be uninvolved. But the likelihood is much greater, since the usual arrangement lends itself so readily to the passive teaching/learning mode that requires students to absorb facts and information. It is also more likely in this setting that students will goof off during class—especially if it is a large lecture-class situation. Both the students' feeling of boredom with the lecture and the arrangement of the chairs lend themselves to fooling around.

Sean, a 1987 South Lakes graduate, wrote on his alumni survey what often happens in lectures, and the consequences he saw:

> You would not believe the sort of nonsense that goes on in large [lecture] classrooms . . . The main problem with [these] classes is that they are inevitably distracting. Patricia has a date with John this weekend, so Denise and Paul have to talk about it. Blake has to go to the bathroom, so he has to ask the teacher's permission. Beth has her "Walkman" . . . with the headphones [on] . . . the teacher can't hear the music but everyone within 10 yards can hear it. You know what I'm talking about. Some teachers could control large classes, but most couldn't, and would struggle through each period, getting worn down with every bell, until by the end of the day the wrinkles and hoarse voice gave in to dismay and defeat. I really don't know how teachers remain calm, and why in the world they continue teaching. Some don't remain calm and shout at their students. Of course, this only makes matters worse. The class then becomes a game to see how far we can push before the teacher explodes. It is a mystery to me how I came out of South Lakes with any knowledge besides who got drunk last weekend at Charles' party.

Moreover, this situation makes it much easier for the teacher to become the font of all wisdom,—and, as Sean indicated, power and authority. Or, as another student said on a 1990 government course evaluation, the best learning situation in high school was being "in an open circle with the teacher sitting with us, not standing up in front of class dictating authority."

Not magic

Putting the chairs in a circle is not magic. It does not cure all problems. There still are students who do not like the circle because it does make it hard to hide. It is easy for Johnny or Suzie, sitting in rows, to slink down in a chair behind a desk at the back of the room and hope that the teacher doesn't call on them or even notice them. Of course, this sometimes happens even in the circle. A few kids find it hard to break the habit of trying to hide as they do in conventional classroom arrangements, and pull their chairs back from the circle.

But such behavior reflects the very boredom and lack of involvement in learning that is generally reinforced by the row arrangement. It can also reflect student fears of being belittled by the teacher for not knowing something or not having done assigned work. Again, the circle does not preclude this from happening, but it makes it much less likely. When the teacher uses the circle as a learning environment in which kids are involved, are not bored, feel safe, and do not fear belittlement, then the very behaviors exhibited in the standard classroom arrangement tend to disappear. Both students and teacher feel better about the situation and about each other because it is an open, mutually supportive environment.

The general lack of using a circle in high schools also shows what many think of as "hard" learning. After all, children in elementary schools sometimes sit in circles for activities, so it is not as if the idea were completely new. Unfortunately, most high school teachers seem to think that, besides creating a danger of losing control, the circle makes it harder to be what they think of as serious. But that is simply not so. If the teacher sets a tone of seriousness-of-purpose as well as of warmth and caring, genuinely serious learning can take place. As one student said on a 1990 government course evaluation about serious learning and the role of the circle:

> The classroom environment has been superb! The circle setup that you have used is very effective . . . The students are so incredibly informed and involved and we are dying of thirst for knowledge. I have become politically aware, and much more interested.

Here is a comment about the value of the circle made by Aretha, an 11th grade student in an American history class taught in the 1985–86 school year. Aretha was an intelligent young woman for whom school had frequently been an unsuccessful experience:

> If it wasn't for the class being in a circle and communicating among each other, I would not know as much as I do. If we just sat in desks in your class and did assignments, I would know nothing because I'd either not do them or just daydream.

The circle, then, is a technique to be used as part of creating a learning environment in which kids are encouraged to become involved, to think and to question—and to see that other students and not just the teacher or the textbook have knowledge and insights to share. As yet another student wrote on a 1990 government course evaluation:

> The arrangement of the chairs [in a circle] is beneficial to us, so we can listen to one another. This allows us to step out of ourselves and focus on what other people are saying and [on] their ideas.

Other techniques

There are other good learning techniques that contribute to providing good education. These include having students work in small groups, study independently, plan and participate in individual field trips, and participate in purposeful, well-planned group field trips. As with the circle, these provide opportunities for students to grow and learn. They also encourage students to test taking charge of their own learning and growth. There is some discussion of these in later parts of the book.

The Problem

4

Authower

During my final year of teaching this word was accidentally coined by one of my students and me. In a class discussion one day, at the same moment that I said the word *authority* Melanie Kammerling said *power*. And what came out of our mouths was *Authower!*

The watchword

Authower is a watchword. The meaning is as darkly negative as it sounds. Authower refers to the abuse of authority and power by those in positions of leadership. It is everywhere —in politics, in bureaucracies, in the business world, in schools. Lord Acton was right about power corrupting, even in a democratic society.[1] And in a democracy the only defense against Authower is for those affected by it to learn how to counter it and limit it, to make it accountable to them. Authority and power should be no more than are necessary to perform the legitimate tasks of governance, including education.

Teachers and administrators too frequently embody Authower. There simply are too many teachers (and administrators) who are petty and sometimes downright mean.

When teachers set rigid rules that fail to account for student foible and error, and penalize students unfairly and unnecessarily, that is Authower. When teachers do not demonstrate respect for the students as people, belittling them and their ideas, that is Authower. When teachers get angry and intolerant if students do not do assigned work, failing to take into account that students have many needs, concerns and frustrations that may, in *their* minds, take precedence over schoolwork, that is Authower. When teachers get unnecessarily angry when students are late to class, or turn work in late, and become punitive and sarcastic, that is Authower.

In these kinds of situations, teachers are acting not out of concern for students but out of an often unrecognized, unacknowledged need to be in charge. These actions reveal a deep level of insecurity and anger, which takes itself out in harsh, counterproductive behavior with kids. Often teachers justify these kinds of behaviors as necessary to maintain control and to force students to learn. Actually, most of the time one of two things happens in response to Authower. Some students cave in resentfully, doing whatever the teacher wants to get a grade, and then forget most of what was supposedly learned as soon as the class is over or the assignment completed. Other students rebel in self-defeating ways. They act out their anger and further widen the gulf between the teacher and themselves, and learn nothing.

Teachers easily get caught up in trivia, and too often can't or don't see the forest for the trees. The rules they think they are supposed to enforce, or the need many feel to force students to learn, often blind teachers to the complexities of the teaching/ learning process. Few teachers are deliberately mean for the sake of being mean, but students are not in a position to see the subtle differences between deliberate and non-deliberate meanness.

There is something about traditional teaching in a traditional school building that lends itself to Authower. By traditional teaching is meant a teacher-centered classroom where the teacher is dominant at all times. In this kind of class, all information flows from teacher to student, rarely from student to student or from student to teacher. There is seldom any interaction, any discussion among members of the class or with the teacher. With that kind of classroom approach, a teacher in a traditional building can shut the door to the room and become Authower.

Years ago I heard the phrase, "the classroom teacher, like the captain of a ship, is one of the few remaining absolute monarchs on this earth." What an entree to Authower! But as a beginning teacher, I, too, fell into the Authower trap. In my attempt to establish the control I thought I needed over the students in my first year of teaching, I used to quote that phrase to the kids. Looking back, I don't know how many of my students really understood what that meant, but they all surely understood the authoritarian behavior that went with it. And saying that to the kids made me feel good at the time!!

To some extent teacher Authower is also a consequence of teaching in the hectic, nonstop environment of most public high schools and is a response to the often petty rules of the system. Trying to handle all of this causes many teachers to become uptight, helping to produce Authower. This is not an excuse for Authower, but it is part of the explanation.

A hard judgement

Administrator Authower also is partly a consequence of the nature of the high school world. Principals and assistant principals most often come into contact with students who get in trouble and are sent to their offices: the students who don't comply with teachers' (or the school's) rules and expectations, or those who are just plain goof-offs. The kids who get in trouble most often are the academically unsuccessful students. Working infrequently with the academically successful students, the so-called "good kids," school administrators often become cynical, often lose perspective. Too many lapse into Authower. In the 1985 movie, *The Breakfast Club,* a central character was an assistant principal supervising five students who were serving detention for an entire Saturday for having broken various school rules. The portrayal of the assistant principal as a fool, as Authower, was only a slight exaggeration of far too many school administrators.

This is a hard judgement about teachers and administrators, but it is sadly accurate. Moreover, it is supported by the consistent and frequent comments about petty and hurtful behavior by teachers and administrators from a wide variety of students and former students over three decades.

Ask a student about any course and the first thing you will be told about is whether the teacher is mean or nice, understanding or not, helpful or not. For virtually all students, the value of a course is measured by their perception of the teacher. That is about as close to a universal truth in the game of school as one can get. Moreover, for most students the issue is not only whether they like the teacher as a person but whether they see the teacher as competent, whether they respect the teacher. Teachers play a central role in the education of students. Students almost universally equate the value of a course with their perception of the teacher. It is vital to understand that if schools are to become more effective as places where kids can learn and grow, teacher (and administrator) Authower must be seen and addressed seriously as a major problem.

Teachers and administrators do not have to be Authower. If teachers, especially, were trained effectively to be more involved, and if they *were* more involved in developing and deciding educational policies and procedures, their need to be Authower would be less. If the system encouraged and supported their involvement, they would be secure with the whole process. Teachers need to be taught to work with and be comfortable with parent and student involvement in policy and school procedures of decision-making.

Parental involvement helps

Parents should be involved in school affairs all the time, not just when their children are in trouble. Their presence could limit Authower or even prevent it from developing. Yes, parents do try to become involved They may act as room mothers and coordinators of voluntary activities. In many school systems parents serve on curriculum advisory committees and on textbook adoption committees. But at the high school level this kind of parent involvement is, for the most part, just window-dressing. It gives the illusion that parents are involved while it prevents them from being *meaningfully* involved or asking too many questions. It's akin to throwing a bone to a dog to keep it quiet.

In other words, parents are co-opted rather than actually planning courses and helping teach them. Parents can serve as mentors for students, or even as employers of students who are in apprentice-like situations. Parents should be strongly encouraged to spend time in schools, visit classes, make suggestions, and get to know the teachers (and the students) as people. This is necessary and possible, and would contribute greatly to curbing Authower.

Who is school supposed to benefit?

Above all else, students—the customers, the reason we have schools in the first place—must be intimately and actively involved in the process of their own education. This, too, would limit Authower.

Kids should be involved in school decisions. Teachers should be more involved than they are now. That is not to say that either should be in total control. But high school students shouldn't just accept teacher or administrator authority blindly, or rebel against it ineffectively. They can learn to question, to define their own goals, and to share in determining their own educational destinies, appropriate to their varying developmental levels and individual interests. There is every reason why high school students should have a voice, yes, have some power over their own education.

Even bright high school seniors know amazingly little about how the school system is run and who makes decisions. Students are rarely informed of the reasons for rules, or changes in them. Students don't know who makes decisions or rules. Often they don't realize that many rules and regulations are made by the school board for the whole school system, or are the result of state laws, and are not simply an individual school's rules. This latter point is especially important, for often when students get upset about some school rule they spin their wheels blaming the wrong culprit. Students must be helped to understand that laws and school board policies, even many individual school rules, are the result of complex political actions by conflicting interest groups.

Students' lack of knowledge about how the system works is an example of the system's tendency to keep everyone at bay. After twelve years of this pattern, students stop trying to find out how and why the system works. They accept school as a given. Any curiosity they had about how and why it functions has been wiped out well before their senior year of high school. Students' acceptance of how the system works is a passive resignation that breeds alienation and discontent, not the wise acceptance of situations that cannot be altered, such as rain forcing the cancellation of a planned outdoor event.

Part of involving students in decisions about their own education would be encouraging them learn about how and why schools function as they do. For the system this would be risky, even dangerous. If students *did* understand more about the how and why of schools, they would not only be in a position to limit Authower—or at least limit its impact on them personally—they would raise questions that might be very hard for the system to answer. After I became aware of how prevalent is student ignorance of the way the system works, I usually spent some time in each class each year acquainting my students with the reality of school politics.

Power corrupts

It must be acknowledged that there is a kind of satisfaction for the person who has Authower and uses it. No doubt that is a big part of the psychological basis for the corrupting characteristics of power. In this way it is not unlike a drug habit. The habit is ultimately disastrous for the addict, but being under the influence usually feels great! That is the seductive quality of addiction. Authower is similarly seductive—and similarly harmful both to those who exercise it and to their victims. And no one can more easily fall into the trap of addiction to Authower than teachers.

Why? Outside of prison guards, it is hard to imagine another group of people who have the kind of daily responsibility for and power over an essentially powerless (and captive) group than do teachers. Moreover, an unintended by-product of American public schools is a strong tendency for teachers to feel insecure. There are four sources for this feeling:

- The very public, fishbowl characteristic of public school teaching.

- The lack of control over their professional circumstances.

- Inadequate training and system support on the job.

- An unnecessarily helpless response to these other factors.

A good support system would encourage teachers to be creative, to take risks. Instead, the system supports teachers who do not challenge, who take no risks, and who, therefore, do not create an exciting learning environment for kids. No wonder such a vast number of high school students feel boredom and alienation.

So Authower is a way of controlling all these negatives. If teachers cannot control their professional environment, if they do not acknowledge or even recognize why they feel harried and unsatisfied with the job, if they feel angry when students do not behave as they think students should, if they feel insecure and powerless, then their frequent response is to become Authower. This may be unconscious. Teachers who embody Authower would deny it and see themselves in a more angelic light—or at the very least, see themselves as martyrs to the cause of educating our youth. But Authower is lurking there and exercising its destructive force. The institutional forces that help create Authower need to be addressed. But teachers themselves need to acknowledge its existence and understand its causes. Teachers (or administrators) will not be Authower when they no longer feel the need to be.

Notes

1. "Power tends to corrupt and absolute power corrupts absolutely," Lord Acton, in a letter to Bishop Mandell Greighton, April 5, 1887; *Bartlett's Familiar Quotations*, 15th edition, Little Brown, and Company, Boston, 1980, p.615.

5

The Lego Model of Education

A century after John Dewey and the other leaders of the progressive education movement began the modern school revolution, there still is a widely-held image of high school that is set in the 19th century. The image is largely accurate. I call it the Lego®[1] model of education.

Lego building blocks are interchangeable. Children can easily construct a wide variety of buildings with them. If you lose one Lego brick you just replace it with another. And when all the bricks fit in the correct way, there is a finished product. This seems to be the image most people have of school.

Using Lego bricks is a great activity for children—it makes sense. But using the Lego model for education does not.

The Lego model of education says that the purpose of school is to produce a product: an "educated" student. To do this the teacher lectures—talks at—the kids for 40 to 60 minutes. Sometimes the kids take notes on what is said or copy what is put on the board. Sometimes the teacher asks questions and elicits answers from the kids. Sometimes the kids ask their own questions. Sometimes kids work at their desks reading in a textbook and answering questions at the end of the chapter (seat work) while the teacher walks around the room to check on the work, or to help. Other times, the teacher sits at his or her desk and corrects papers or reads a book while the kids do the seat work. An unconscious image many folks have of a high school classroom is a stereotypical history class, with the teacher at the front of the room lecturing and the kids at their desks taking notes (or pretending to).Occasionally, a really lively teacher will point to a wall map to illustrate a point made in the lecture.

If all classes operate the same way then students can move from one to the other and fit in like a Lego brick. If Tate is transferred from Ms. Tompkin's government class, period 3, to Mr. Alloya's class, period 5, there is no problem of adjustment for him: Tompkin and Alloya are doing the same thing with the same basic assignments.

Fit tab a into slot a

When students are absent, making up what was missed is just a matter of fitting in the right bricks. If Loretta is absent for a few days, and her parents request her assignments to do at home, the assumption is that there are busywork-type assignments that can be sent home for her to do: work sheets or questions at the back of textbook chapters. It is easy on everyone. The teacher can easily write on a form: "Do Chapter 15 questions." The student can do the assignment with little thought. The parents are satisfied with this kind of school work.

The popular image of a high school classroom holds the desks and chairs in rows, facing the chalkboard. The teacher stands in front of the board, facing the rows of students.

In the Lego model the teacher "teaches" and the student "learns." You "know" that students have learned because they have passed tests. It is all cut and dried and mercifully unambiguous—like building with Lego bricks.

Indeed, most of high school education *is* based on the Lego model. Student comments throughout my teaching career over three decades support this allegation. They say that most regular academic classes are conducted in this interchangeable brick fashion. In her alumni survey response, Janice, a 1988 South Lakes graduate quoted previously, compared the typical high school class to a cattle car:

> . . . classes in which the teacher adopted a cattle-car attitude- "get'em in, get'em out." In these situations the defined student/teacher role made the learning experience seem almost hostile— i.e., the teacher was obligated to ram as much of a textbook down a student's throat [as possible] and the student was obligated to regurgitate that same textbook [on a test]. This sort of ram rod philosophy naturally creates an antagonistic relationship between the teacher and student, thereby smothering any meaningful absorption of material on the student's part and any positive feedback for which the teacher may have hoped.

But teaching and learning do not *have* to be based on the Lego model. In an environment where students are encouraged to be self-directed, education is a flowing experience for students and teachers. For enhanced teaching and learning, substitute a river for the Lego bricks. On the flowing river, participants in the teaching-learning process (teachers and students) move along at varying paces, stopping at different points along the way to come ashore and experience what is available. Janice put it this way, continuing her comments above:

> There were . . . exceptions . . . All were situations in which I verbally, mentally, and physically participated in the class and came away with a true feeling of having learned (ah, the magic word) something . . . Very few teachers in high school take the time and energy to allow—no, encourage—the kind of interaction so common in your classes. It is the two-way education that is most effective. The evidence is clear to me. I know what works and what doesn't: boredom kills all desire for knowledge. High school, for the most part, was unbearably boring. Case closed.

During an audio-taped conversation in May 1990, Jeremy, a 1990 South Lakes graduate, described the usual classroom situation as "rushing the information" past the students thus:

> I think looking back there's only a few classes where that [rushing . . .] hasn't been an issue . . . I mean most of the educational system is like that, the teachers are like, "why do I have to teach this? Because this is what the School Board says I have to teach and so I gotta get through this, this year—I got all this other stuff to do." So it's zoom, zoom, zoom . . . Just know it for the test, get the good grade, you're out . . . I think in your class the atmosphere is set so that, I mean, well, let's put it this way: everyone shines and you learn not just from you but from all the other kids . . . I think what your class forces everyone to have is their own responsibilities—[like] they're going to have to face in college . . .

Substitute teachers—sub plans

Teachers as well as students are limited by the Lego model of education. For instance, teachers are required to provide lessons for substitute teachers—sub plans, as they're often called. The Lego model predicates that teachers, like building bricks, are interchangeable parts. If Teacher A can't come to school one day, she or he can be replaced by Substitute A and the teacher's classes will go right on almost as if nothing had happened. This view *might* be valid if all the teacher did was administer lesson plans as one would administer cough syrup to a sick child. In that case, a reasonably intelligent sub could do the same thing. But this is not valid. Even poor teachers interact with kids in some way, and alter their plans in an almost infinite variety of ways during the day. The lesson plan is a general guide, a set of reminders. Of course, the degree and quality of interaction between teacher and students, and the teacher's dependence on the lesson plan, vary among teachers. Nonetheless, it is crazy to assume that a substitute can meaningfully replace a teacher, especially since subs are usually called to school on the morning of the day the teacher is out.

In many high schools teachers are asked to leave at the school a set of all-purpose emergency sub plans for their classes in case they cannot get current plans to the school for the day they will be out. But these all-purpose plans are a joke—and only underscore the Lego model premise of the substitute teacher's role. Teachers are still expected to provide current plans even if they are suddenly ill and will likely be out for only a day or two. The quality or value of those plans is not important.

Thus, the fact that the sub is in the class does not mean "learning" goes on as if the teacher were there. The sub is a baby-sitter. The literal lesson plan may or may not be wasted, but certainly the sub cannot provide what the teacher can provide for the students.

So what if the substitute does not teach exactly as the teacher would? Since not all learning stems from the teacher anyway, then perhaps it is good occasionally to introduce a sub to demonstrate another approach, another point of view. But that is not the system's point in having a sub for a teacher. The system's *stated* point is that the students must not miss any "instructional time." Using a sub to provide another viewpoint, new ideas and insights, another adult to question and interact with and, hopefully, enjoy would be honest and useful. It would obviate the game of sub plans. But this is not likely.

Moreover, there is another system reason for subs: they are an administrative convenience. Remember that a very high priority for any school administration is to maintain order. The school must be smoothly-run, with a minimum of problems and, above all, a minimum of complaints, especially from parents. If subs came in just to interact with the kids, to question them and be questioned by them, this could be risky—or so the administration fears. What if a parent calls and asks why Maria did not have her math lesson today? Or why Harry didn't have his French lesson today? No, rather than risk dealing with that, the system says it is better to continue the fiction that the regular lesson has been administered to the kids whether or not the regular teacher is there. The system says it is better to force teachers to participate in the game of school by submitting sub plans.

Eliminating subs

There is at least one alternative that has been tried in some schools: if the teacher is going to be out just a day or two, and especially if it is a last-minute, unexpected absence, why not eliminate the sub altogether? A notice could be put at the entrance to the teacher's room that she or he will be out that day and give places for students to go during that period: the library, a tutorial room, a commons area, a study hall, etc.

This system would even work with 9th grade students, let alone with seniors, if they were taught self-discipline, and self-direction, and if they were excited about learning and felt a part of the school. High school-age students are quite capable of self-directing themselves to select one of the alternatives to the classroom room for a day or two.[2]

So, the Lego model of education is stifling. It discourages creativity and spontaneity. It cripples the development of thinking, caring, questioning and knowledgeable adults who can function effectively in our complex technological age and in a pluralistic, democratic society. It *may* have been appropriate for the 19th century. It is totally inappropriate for the 20th and 21st centuries.

But like an old shoe, the Lego model is very comfortable for many folks. It is a known entity. It does not require new energy or thought. For teachers, administrators, school board members and students it is safe precisely because it is familiar. The Lego model is also safe because it is known and understood by parents and the general public. It is comfortable for teacher training colleges. Though, to their credit, many teacher training programs do introduce prospective teachers to new methods and ideas, for the most part they are part of the system. They avoid using their influence to move schools away from the Lego model. It is easier and safer that way.

Moreover, the Lego model allows schools to appear to respond to criticism or demands for change without actually doing much at all. If learning is just a matter of fitting the right bricks together, then responding to criticism is just a matter of replacing defective bricks. Schools are good at adopting superficial solutions that seem to respond to criticism but actually change little or nothing because they only tinker with the system. Solutions that leave the basic structure that produced the criticisms in the first place in place are like sticking an arm or a leg on a clay figure after the body has been formed.

Moulding results

Children learn that if they want a clay figure to hold together they should mould it from one piece of clay. Arms, legs, neck, head, and the body, all should be squeezed out of one piece of clay. That way the figure is much less likely to fall apart. Without learning the word *organic,* children learn the concept that word implies while learning how to make clay figures: to solve problems effectively, they must be dealt with as a whole. That is, problems must be dealt with in the context of their underlying causes and their relationship to the structure and environment of which they are a part. To do otherwise will achieve the same kind of result as adding an arm to an already-formed clay body: the arm may stick for a while, but before long it will fall off and a new solution to the armless body problem will have to be found. This is a lesson that schools seem not to have learned, perhaps do not want to learn.

Instead, schools keep adding arms and legs to a body that was formed long along. Schools keep trying superficial, non-organic solutions that do not address fundamental causes. And they keep coming up short. The sub plans requirement is an example of a non-organic way schools handle a problem. And quick-fix responses to concern over low academic achievement of minority students and students from economically poor homes is another. For instance, often schools will institute some special program that appears to address the concern but fails to achieve the desired results.

This is not because the students are stupid but because the underlying reasons for their poor achievement are the result of many factors the schools generally ignore: the poor training and attitudes of the teaching staff, the continued use of inappropriate teaching techniques that insure failure, the lack of intelligent involvement of the kids' families, and the negative impact on the kids of television and the materialism of American society. Kids from economically depressed environments are even more vulnerable to seduction by the material glitz of TV than are more affluent kids. The affluent ones may accept the schools' line that if they do well academically in school they will achieve the goodies on display. There is no particular reason for poor kids to accept this line, especially if the adults they see around them (drug dealers and others) seem to have the goodies without the academic achievement.

Kids may not have an accurate perception of the value of academic achievement, but it is a perception that is difficult to correct simply by imposing a special program on them out of the context of the rest of their world. The problem with schools is not that they try to impose special programs out of context but that they fail to show that, without taking into account that context, the programs are doomed to failure. But this would require a kind of honesty and openness that public schools seldom exhibit.

The quantitative model

The movement for increasing the school day and year is another example of schools responding to concerns with superficial, inappropriate solutions. This challenge, however, is based on the alter ego of the Lego model, the *quantitative* model, which says that more is better. The movement is a response to horror stories in the press that American kids aren't learning as much as they should; certainly not as much as Japanese or European students.

The invidious comparison to Japanese or European schools completely fails to consider the critical cultural factors that make American society and its schools very different from Japan or Europe. Think of the diverse population in the United States. Think of the value system of this country, which places excessive emphasis on the acquisition of private gain and on individualism. Think of the extreme affluence and contrasting great poverty, and the "need" for instant gratification developed by the market place in order to sell products to youth—the essence of the artificially created teenager. Think of the more rigid school systems in most other countries with their specialization at a young age and limited opportunity to change paths. Think of the incredible pressure on Japanese kids to succeed. Think of the fact there is a much stronger commitment in this country than in most other countries to educating *everyone*. The very notion of a *public* school system in the U.S. is that the school is open to the entire public.[3]

Legal and political battles

There is a history in America of legal and political battles over questions of access to public education. In the 1870's a series of state supreme court decisions held that public money could be used to finance public high schools (this having generally been established already for public elementary schools). The most famous was the Kalamazoo decision by the Michigan Supreme Court in 1872. Starting in the 1930's, a series of court challenges to racially segregated public schools culminated in the great 1954 *Brown v. Board of Education* decision in which the U.S. Supreme Court ruled unanimously that racial segregation in public schools is unconstitutional. There have been legal and political battles throughout the American experience over the right of states to compel attendance at school. By now, virtually every state requires students to be in school until at least age 16, and there is great economic and social pressure for students to graduate from high school. In spite of increased drop-out rates in some areas, overall high school graduation rates are high.

We have fought long and hard in the United States to establish the notion that everyone should to go school. As Ken Plum said,[4] "we [the public schools] have to take every kid who comes down the pike." Indeed, it is this very commitment to try to educate everyone that provides strong support for the Lego/quantitative model of schools. It is much easier to educate everyone (or seem to do so), to try to get all kids through high school, if we stick with a system that tries to put all kids in the same mold whether or not they can or should fit.

What this means for comparisons to other countries is that there is in America a far wider, more varied and less selective sampling of students whose test results are compared to those of a much smaller and generally more selective sampling of students in most other countries. And all this takes place in the context of a society in which students are hyped on instant gratification and material acquisitions. These same kids are often denied necessary support from adults who are preoccupied with such pressures as job insecurity, long commuting hours, and isolation from extended family and community and their own desire for instant gratification. No wonder they pay little attention to their children. But this makes serious academic achievement all the more difficult.

American schools—American values

The American system of education is a reflection of American values and patterns just as the values of other countries are reflected in their education systems. Without a radical change in basic societal values and practices, trying to adopt Japanese or European education systems in the United States would be like sticking the arm to that clay figure after making the body. Or it would mean trying to replace defective bricks with new ones without examining the foundation that supports the whole building.

The idea of an increased school day and year is a direct outgrowth of the quantitative and Lego model mentality. The catch phrase is "more instructional time." This clever political carrot appeals to a common fallacy about teaching and learning: that learning is a static thing to be administered by teachers to students. Like piling bricks one on the other to make a wall, the more time teachers have to do the administering, the better. It is sort of like the misconception many people have about taking vitamins. Since one vitamin pill is supposed to be good for you, two must be that much better. But that is not necessarily so. And it most definitely is not so when it comes to education: more of what we have now is not only not better, it is worse. If a longer school day meant a very different kind of learning environment and set of assumptions, then having a longer school day might make sense. But since the call for longer school days and years assumes more of what we have now, this is another example of applying the Lego/quantitative models—and thus does not make sense.

This brings us to the matter of why we have schools, to a definition of good education. If the purpose of a public school system is to lift the tops off students' heads and pour in facts and information, then the concept of "instructional time" *may* make some sense, though I do not think that is the best way of truly learning facts. But that is not what the public schools should be all about. As I keep saying, schools do need to help kids learn information and facts—but not as an end in itself. In keeping with Jefferson's reminder that democracy must have an enlightened populace, the task of schools should be to help young people develop their intellectual and personal potentials. This task is better understood now thanks, in great part, to the Progressives and their successors. But the task has just begun and is not easy. Resistance is high to encouraging kids to think and question. Just look at the prevalence of our 19th century Lego model of education as we approach the 21st century.

Americans have spent far more time discussing the idea of schools than the substance of education and the structure of schools. For the most part, until quite recently, we left it up to professional educators to be concerned with substance and structure. And, for the most part, the educators have been content to stick with the Lego and quantitative models that evolved over the centuries. Why not? It's easier and people are used to it. It's as if we applied to the substance and structure of schools the adage, "if it ain't broke, don't fix it." Well, it *is* broke and it *does* need fixing.

Notes

1. Lego is a Registered Trademark of INTERLEGO A.G.

2. I am limiting my suggestions re: substitutes to high schools, because the circumstances are different with younger kids. But even here, I cannot believe that a better system of providing for kids when the regular teacher has to be away for a day or two cannot be found if the system wanted to do so.

3. Cataloging differences between American, European and Japanese schools does not, of course, take into account that the American system tends to give a not very useful general education to millions of kids who have no bridge to the world of work. Nor do the differences with other systems mean that we should not *adapt* some ideas from elsewhere—such as the apprenticeship system in Germany. Indeed, this is consistent with the plans of the Clinton Administration to try to make American education more useful for all students.

4. This is Plum's comment quoted in Chapter 2

The Players

6

Students: We Don't *Have* To Infantilize Them

Students are capable of doing *so much more* learning and growing and, yes, hard work, than they are generally asked to do in high schools. "Hard work" does not mean nightly busy work or six to seven hours a day of boring, tedious classes in school. It means challenging students to think critically, to question intelligently, to be self-directed and self-disciplined, to do worthwhile research, to write more and better, to expand their intellectual horizons, to do useful work. For most students high school learning is listening to the teacher, memorizing the material, and regurgitating it on a test. There is little involvement, little questioning, little expanding of intellectual horizons—and virtually no self-direction.

Students need to be involved in the process of their own learning and growth. They need to see the value and purpose of what they are being asked to do. They need to be so excited about learning that it is not a chore but a satisfying challenge. In addition, they need to be involved in the life of their community and the world. Their formal educational experiences should mesh with the rest of their lives.

Given the degree to which the concepts of involvement, meaningful work and self-direction are ignored in our high schools, one might think they are brand new notions. But they are not. Progressives as far back as John Dewey, beginning at the end of the 19th century, and extending through Alfred North Whitehead and Abraham Maslow and others, have cogently argued for a system of education that starts with the student, not the subject: a system of education that does not merely cram information down students' throats, but encourages students to grab for information, for knowledge, out of their own needs and interests. The basic idea is quite simple: if you start with the needs and feelings of young people as

61

they see themselves, build on what they know and want, and then introduce them to ideas and skills new to them, they are much more likely to buy into what we adults think they should know. They are much more likely to become what they must ultimately become if they truly are to learn: voluntary learners.

Above all else, high school students need to be dealt with seriously as young men and women moving into adulthood. They must not be infantilized. That is, they must not be treated as if they need to be constantly supervised and constantly reminded of what they are supposed to do. They ought to test out things for themselves, learn by trial and error, and then find out that it is ok to slip and fall now and then—that one can learn to get up and carry on.

This does not mean giving young people tasks and responsibilities inappropriate to their age and experience. Nor does it mean that teachers or other adults should abandon kids and just let them run wild. Of course not. Kids, even high school seniors, want support and help from adults. But they want that support and help from adults they trust, adults they feel care about them. Young people do not want adults who manipulate them and arrogantly try to impose their values and beliefs. What kids need are adults who try to see the world through the eyes of the kids, who offer guidance and suggestions after taking into account the needs, feelings and perceptions of the kids.

When I call for involving students in the process of their own learning and encouraging them to be self-directed and independent I am most definitely not advocating a free-for-all situation. In early progressive schools many of the very good ideas of the progressive educators were poorly implemented. Students were turned loose and not given adequate support appropriate to their ages and development. The result was a kind of chaos that Dewey and others did not advocate.

I *am* advocating an environment that challenges students intellectually and also supports their need to grow personally, one being closely linked to the other. For this to happen, students must not merely be allowed but encouraged to be independent and self-directed during their growing up years.

The challenge for teachers and students is to develop together ways of helping students grow and learn, and become independent and self-directed. This is an on-going process. What different students can and will do varies, of course. The starting point of the process, the framework in which the process takes place, must be an articulated, understood assumption that high school-age young people *can* develop intellectually and personally more fully than they generally are encouraged or even permitted to do in schools. Given this, the possibilities for genuine student growth and learning are virtually limitless.

Self-directed study

I began to understand all this at Northport High School in 1961. The school had just begun an unusual program for students called SEDS: Self-Directed Study. The brain-child of David Allardice, then the principal of Northport, and William Duncan, a math teacher at the school, SEDS provided a way for students to use school time to learn on their own about any topic of interest to them. Here was the opposite of infantilizing students: strongly encouraging of them to learn to function as independent, responsible people.

As SEDS was developed under its first director, Bruce Hunt, then a social studies teacher at the school, it was open to any student. Though the majority of the participating students probably were the stronger academic students, as SEDS became better known an increasing number of poorer academic students did SEDS projects. Indeed, many of the very best academic students, who sometimes are called grade grubs, did not do a SEDS project for fear of taking time away from getting good grades.

There were no prerequisites to doing a SEDS project. There was no minimum grade point average required. The only limit as to topic was what might be imposed by the lack of available facility or equipment in the school. In fact, projects were incredibly varied, ranging from esoteric studies of literature or history to gymnastics to designing mechanical objects to painting and sculpting to preparing for college admissions and future careers. Interested students only had to fill out a simple application declaring their desire to start a SEDS project and stating the general topic area; a specific goal or a thesis was not required. Students also had to have parental permission to participate, and they were required to have a short meeting with the SEDS director and the principal to explain their projects. After that, the student was in SEDS. Students also had to find teacher-consultants to whom they could go for help.

The term "teacher-consultant" was deliberate. These teachers were not advisors. They were willing adults to whom students could go for help and support about their SEDS projects but only if they felt the need. If a student did not want to meet with his or her consultant, that was fine. However, the agreement usually reached between teacher-consultants and students assumed that the student was making contact with the teacher periodically. The consultant did not check up on the student, although, according to Hunt, "periodically I would ask the teachers if they were in contact with the kid."[1] As it turned out, most students did periodically meet with their consultants, some more often than others.

The SEDS project received no grade. It was not a part of the student's official transcript. A letter about the student's project was placed in his or her file. Students could use this as a part of their college or job applications and could ask their teacher/consultants to be references. Participation in a SEDS project was intended to be its own reward; anything else was frosting on the cake.

There was no requirement for students to turn in any kind of a final paper or report. They could end their SEDS project whenever they wanted to. Some worked on their projects for less than a semester. Some continued for more than one school year. Some worked during the summer vacation. Students were asked to complete short questionnaires when they ended their projects, though this was not a requirement, and some participated in audio-taped evaluation discussions.

A central component of SEDS was the right of students to take off from any class to work on their projects. There was no limit to the number of classes that could be missed, though students were not supposed to miss pre-announced tests unless they first checked with the teacher. Otherwise, students did not have to get teacher permission to miss any class. They simply put their names on the daily SEDS list indicating which classes they were not attending that day. They did not have to say why or offer any explanation. The student *was* obligated to find out what went on in the class missed, or to check ahead of time with the teacher, and deal with it appropriately, whether this meant making up an assignment or whatever. In other words, a student doing a SEDS project still had to keep up with the regular class work. The point was to provide a way for students to learn to manage their own time, direct their own study, and to learn-by-doing (in the best tradition of Dewey and the others) to establish their own priorities. They were provided in-school time to work on their projects, to build into their school day a time and space for them to do this learning.

The major hurdles that SEDS faced were the conflicts that arose over the right of students to miss virtually any class they wanted in order to work on their projects. Many of the teachers disliked this. Some teachers believed that a student could not possibly learn classroom material and get a good grade without regular class attendance. These teachers felt that when a student missed a class for any reason it was a disaster, though missing class for what were perceived as legitimate reasons (such as illness) was not as bad. Other teachers resented the right of students to determine for themselves whether to attend class. Though few teachers would admit it, the students' right to do this was threatening. It flew directly in the face of teacher authority—of Authower.

Goofing off

Certainly there were teachers who were supportive of SEDS, who did not hassle the kids when they missed class, who were willing to be teacher-consultants. But even many of these teachers had a hard time with the fact that sometimes kids would miss a class for SEDS and not actually work on their projects in any obvious, direct way. They might "goof off" in some way—looking through magazines in the library, talking to people, sitting somewhere in the building and thinking. One student, Sam, said in an audio-taped discussion in 1964 evaluating the SEDS experience of several students, that though he "took off [from all his classes] every Friday . . . on certain Fridays I just wandered around the school. And on other Fridays you don't even leave the room [where he was working on his project] at all. It depends. Sometimes you feel like staying there all day [and working]."

It is difficult for many people to see the value of allowing students the opportunity to "waste" time in this way. But this is important to understand. If SEDS was a way for students to learn by doing, part of this process was the opportunity, the right, to goof off now and then and learn and see what happens: was it good for me? Was it valuable? Could I have done something else? Do I need to goof off now and then? There are people who do not allow themselves goof-off time. But other folks do need this time occasionally. It is part of life, part of learning. It often is a necessary time for recharging one's batteries, for the brain to think unconsciously, without pressure, particularly if one genuinely *chooses* to goof off.

I am not suggesting that students be actively encouraged to goof-off, nor did the SEDS program do that. But if students are to be encouraged to learn-by-doing as SEDS did, then part of that experience for many is the opportunity to goof-off sometimes. I know of no SEDS student who goofed off all the time.

Some teachers (and parents) also had a hard time understanding students who would choose not to work on SEDS for a long time, or would decide to stop working on it for various reasons sooner than they had planned to, or before they had "finished." What these people were failing to see was that SEDS was a process, not a product. And the common denominator was student self-direction. Whether the student decided to goof off or miss certain classes and not others or stop work on the project altogether, the issue was: this is the student's genuine choice. In 1964, during one of the taped SEDS evaluation discussions, Bruce Hunt said this to a student who was being apologetic for having ended work on his project earlier than planned:

> You may think you rate your project not too successful because you stopped, but . . . at least it had one important element of success, that you were directing it and chose to stop. I don't know if you were wise to stop but . . . you made this decision to stop so you directed your own study . . . even if it's directing it to a grinding halt . . . you stopped and concentrated on your other work to finish up high school in your junior year. It was *your* choice.

Many students felt conflicts over missing classes to work on their projects. There were complaints that quite a few teachers penalized them in various ways when they missed a class for SEDS. Students said some teachers belittled them when they returned to class after having missed the previous day or more to work on their SEDS projects. Students also said that some teachers made it difficult or impossible for them to make up work missed, although teachers were not supposed to penalize kids who missed classes for SEDS. Here is what Rod said during a 1964 audio-taped SEDS evaluation discussion:

> I have two teachers, one an English teacher who is very sarcastic in his remarks, and a math teacher who really likes to come on with quips about me. Like yesterday I came into English class and I hadn't gone Friday, and Monday I was on a field trip [with another class], so we had a test yesterday and he comes onto me with a statement saying, "Ooo, glad to see you are here. It's too bad you came in on the wrong day for the test." Every time I go into this class after I take off a day for SEDS he makes quips and everything. So it really kind of makes me think twice before I take off a day for SEDS and when I do I usually go to the English class because I do not want to make the teacher think that I am taking this because I want to miss his class. So I [often] just go to his class and take off the others.

At any one time no more than about 10% of the student body participated in SEDS. This was not by design but is what happened. Partly this shows that many students simply felt no need to do a SEDS project. But discussions with other students revealed that quite a few would like to have done a SEDS project but were afraid. Some students feared that negative teacher reaction might jeopardize their grades. Some students just were not willing to take the risk of working independently with no supervision, even if the idea appealed to them.

There *was* a risk in participating in SEDS, and that has to do with the real purpose of the SEDS program. It was not the projects themselves, important to the students as they might be. What SEDS provided was an opportunity for students to test out functioning as self-directed people, to plan their own activities and take responsibility for their own decisions and actions. SEDS provided a way, in a sense forced students, to learn-by-doing how to manage conflicts with time, and conflicts with authority.

If a student's work in a scheduled class suffered because of taking off too much time from that class to work on her or his SEDS project, the student had to deal with that. If students felt that they could not take off time from certain classes and thus had to skimp on the SEDS project, they also had to deal with that. When teachers became angry with students who missed class to work on SEDS, the student had to deal with this also. Planning a SEDS project forced students to think carefully about what was really important to them and why, and to act accordingly. This is a lesson many adults have not learned well. For high school students to begin to learn it is valuable indeed.

SEDS not only provided an opportunity for students to test out self-direction, it also stimulated students into thinking about education, schools and learning in general. This 1964 audio-taped discussion with SEDS students gives a glimpse not only of differing student perceptions about SEDS but also differing perceptions about the value of self-direction generally:

Bruce Hunt: How would you rate the SEDS program?

Gail: I don't find anything wrong with the program. I think it is good. You can start and stop whenever you please.

Hunt: Would you rather have a teacher say, "March 30 is the last day you work on SEDS?"

Gail: Oh, no! Because I don't like to think I have to do this, and I don't like to be made to feel I have to do something.

Hunt: Well, what makes you do it [the SEDS project]? Why do you do it?

Gail: I do it because it is something I want to do. It's just something I feel I want to do, and if someone doesn't tell me I have to do this thing, well then it is ok. . . . [in] college, you only have certain days with classes . . . I like that . . . [like] . . . with the government class the way Mr. Tripp conducts his.[2] You only have certain days and you only have certain things you have to do by certain dates . . . I think that is good, it helps me I think with the SEDS project, too.

Hunt: Do you think this [SEDS] could be extended in school or do you think there is not enough direction for the regular school program?

Gail: I think the SEDS program could be more, somehow interwoven with the school subjects. You know, you pick out a subject you want to continue with. I don't know how they could do it . . . work the way you want and you know.

Ted: I tend to disagree with Gail. I think that you would want to do a project [in SEDS] that doesn't have to do with school, that you'd want to learn something outside of school, that you'd want to donate your own time to and that you're very interested in.

Hunt: You're saying extending it, aren't you, Gail? Not replacing it but extending it [i.e., the school subject].

Gail: No, not really. What I mean is like, you have the different courses and instead of having a teacher tell you, well you have to do this and you have to do that, you go off on your own on it.

Hunt: Don't you think the kids would just sit back and goof off?

Gail: No, I feel that if they're interested in the subject enough, without having this constant supervision, they'll go off on their own because they know they have to do this to learn. Where if you have a teacher always supervising you, you get, I don't know, a sort of closed-in feeling or something. I do, I can't stand to have a teacher over me all the time. It bothers me.

Ted: I agree with her but you can't do this all the time because there are many groups that aren't interested in a subject . . . .last year in history we were given a certain amount of work and were told it had to be completed in a certain amount of time, and as it was a good class most of us completed it, but there's always 15% that fall behind, and those 15% would tend to slow the class down a little.

Hunt: How did these students slow you down?

Ted: Well, the teacher's responsible for so much work to teach the students. Now, if a percentage of the class decides not to do this work, the teacher is going to have to take time out, too, [to catch up these students].

Hunt: Isn't Gail saying that we should make the student responsible and not the teacher to teach a certain amount of work? The teacher would be a . . . guide. . . .

Gail: Yes, a guide . . . like [this one teacher] who gives me TV programs to watch. She doesn't say you have to watch these, but they're just something that might benefit me . . .

Hunt: In a few words, what was best and worst about SEDS?

Gail: Well, I haven't found any worst points in it. And I think the best point that I've found is that you are able to take off on your own and do more or less what you've wanted to do without having someone to guide you and not laying out a plan for you to follow.

Ted: I liked the part when the teacher [the teacher-consultant] suggests what he thinks is the best thing. I think that when you are thinking of doing a SEDS project you should have people who have done it in the past to talk to them, instead of just with your advisor.

Clearly, Ted and Gail had different perceptions and were at different points in their own development. Gail seemed much more ready to take self-directed risks. But Ted *did* try out the idea and warmed to it during the project. His last comment reflects his moving toward a broader view of what is possible in education. That alone made SEDS worthwhile.

The following excerpt from a spring 1967 audio-taped discussion with SEDS students further reveals how they felt about and handled conflicts over time and missing classes:

Hunt: You said you know it was wrong to have taken off classes. Well, you took off. In fact, SEDS allows you, theoretically, to take off any class except if there is a pre-announced test in there. So what was wrong?

Edie: Well, I realize it was wrong because I was causing trouble for other SEDS students. When one person gets in trouble for SEDS the whole SEDS gets put in a bad light. I realized this. And I wasn't really thinking about that when I took off those periods but then my teacher wanted me to be in that class. She knew that I wasn't doing well and she wanted me there. So I realize that it was wrong in taking off this period because actually I was jeopardizing all other SEDS students because I was misusing SEDS.

Tripp: How were you "misusing" it?

Edie: By taking off the period and actually not doing anything. That's the seventh period when . . . it's late in the day . . .

Tripp: If you had taken that period off and . . .

Edie: did something . . .

Tripp: . . . did something directly related to your project, would you have felt the same way?

Edie: Yes, I think I would, because it is an academic subject and you still need it and if I do want to graduate I better show up at that class and . . .

Hunt: So what happened? Did you stop . . .

Edie: Oh, I stopped taking off for SEDS that period. It really didn't prove anything. I still hated math. I find out a different way to get out of class.

Tripp: Did you in fact pass with a 65?

Edie: No, as a matter of fact I passed with a 70! What do you think of that?

Hunt: Very good!! Bud, what thoughts about SEDS for you?

Bud: My project was music appreciation, so for the first month or two I just listened to all kinds of music in the practice room, but then it got hard to get a record player and the music teacher said we [Bud was working with another student on the same SEDS project] had to write a report saying what we did in the practice room, and we got bogged down so we just discussed it mostly [after that]. And we did stuff at home and a couple of times Bruce [the other student] brought in his guitar and we would play something. And we did nothing really, but I got something out of it.

Tripp: What do you mean by "do nothing but you get something out of it?"

Bud: Well, we weren't doing any actual work . . . It was more, it was all fun.

Tripp: What's actual work?

Bud: Something you don't want to do . . . or something like that . . . .We tried to find other rooms to listen to the music in, but we couldn't; if we found one, we'd be kicked out because a teacher wanted to use it . . . .I think there ought to be a SEDS room, with a SEDS record player and a SEDS microphone around.

Hunt: Maude, what's your reaction to SEDS?

Maude: Well, I find when I do go to a certain class that I really detest . . . that I'm not going because somebody said that I had to go. It's because I guess I should go and even if I didn't go often I thought in the back of my mind that I better go, so I did go and then I am accomplishing something. Do you understand what I am saying?

Tripp: Yes, but would you accomplish even more if there were no such thing as SEDS, and you were forced to go 5 times a week?

Maude: No, because I would be forced to go . . .

Hunt: You are forced to go most of the time. You have been for 12 years.

Maude: Well, that's true, too, but I didn't like it and I didn't even know why I went. It's because I was forced to go. . . . [It's better if] you find a reason yourself to go. It's not the same as being told to go.

Tripp: Any last comments about SEDS good or bad?

Maude: I find that once in a while if I take off English my teacher will come around and bring me back in, which I find to be quite disturbing . . .

"Come on there, Let's go, let's move on," she'll say. And here I had signed out for that period.

Hunt: Did you tell the teacher?

Maude: Yes. And she said, "I don't care . . . it's more important that you come here." It seems that her class was exception to the rule.

Edie: I don't think the administration realizes the full value of SEDS . . . .When you are sitting in the Commons and reading . . . that's your SEDS project, God[3] comes down: "All right. Let's move on." You have no place to go . . .

Bud: Yes, the problem with sitting in the Commons is, they pass us . . . one teacher said, "I haven't seen your pass." And I said, "There is no pass in SEDS," and I just walked out of the hall. . . . And if you are just sitting around or walking through the halls you have to go through everything if some teacher sees you.

Edie: I think SEDS is so good if the kids have projects they can get something out of. It's worth everything . . . It's meant a lot to me this year. I'm just beginning to realize what it did for me . . . If you have a desire to learn and you have a desire to create, or such, then that's why there's all good in SEDS; there is no bad. You create the bad for yourself . . . you can only go down so far and it's at that point you say, "Oh, God, I can't go on with this. I gotta go back to class." And then's when you are learning.

Maude: Yes, once I take off a class for SEDS and I come back again, it feels much better.

As the student comments indicate, even participants in SEDS had varying interpretations of it. This is a natural reflection of the fact that we all experience life differently, through our own prisms. Yet there was a common thread: virtually all SEDS students appreciated the opportunity to be self-directed and virtually all felt that learning because one wanted to learn was better than learning because one is forced to learn.

This obvious message is frequently dismissed by educators and others as being impractical. There are things kids must learn, it is said, whether or not they want to learn them. But that is not the point. Of course there are things kids need to learn that at least initially they may not want to learn, or don't see the point of learning. They will at least be *willing* to learn even these things, however, if the reasons for learning them are made clear and if teachers engage students honestly.

The shibboleth among teachers generally over students missing classes is a hindrance to students' being encouraged to be independent and self-directed. In turn, this reflects the assumption that in order to learn, students must be constantly taught or be given information by a teacher and must be constantly under direct teacher supervision. This was evident not only in the SEDS program at Northport High School but in a somewhat similar program that Curry Belfield and I started at South Lakes High in 1985.

Poli Obs

In an effort to get kids to learn self-direction and to get them more involved in learning about the social/political world, we started a program of political observation as a part of the government classes. Nicknamed Poli Obs, the idea was for students to take a day off school and visit some governmental agency or government-related activity—the Congress, a court, a lobbying group, or whatever. South Lakes is a 30–40 minute drive from Washington, D.C. But there were plenty of opportunities for a Poli Obs closer to home. A student could go alone or with a few other students. There would be no teacher or other adult along with them. We would discuss logistics ahead of time with students going on a Poli Obs— location of activity, how to get there, making necessary contacts ahead of time, and so forth. We might help kids find who the contacts might be, but the students had to do the actual contacting and make the necessary appointments for the observation.

What the students observed when on a Poli Obs depended on their interests as they defined them. Often students would go on a Poli Obs as a part of their preparation for a research paper. Each quarter students were required to do at least one independent project or activity outside of the class work common to all. One way of fulfilling this requirement was to go on a Poli Obs. Regardless of the purpose of the Poli Obs, students had to submit a written report of their experience.

As might be expected, at first students were hesitant to take advantage of the opportunity Poli Obs afforded them. For most students, going on an individual field trip with no teacher supervision was a new experience. Part of the hesitation was simply fear of the unknown. For a few it seemed like a lot of bother. For some, it was difficult because they had after school jobs. Fulfilling their job responsibility meant cutting down the length of time they had available to get to and from their observation. This was especially difficult if they were going in to Washington to watch Congress or meet with a lobbyist, or whatever. For almost all the students the biggest hurdle was the fear of other teachers' reactions to their missing classes.

Prior to going on a Poli Obs, students had to bring in a signed parent permission form and had to have all their other teachers sign another form which accompanied a brief description of what Poli Obs was all about. Curry and I had already obtained the permission of the school administration to run the program.

One of the learning experiences for the kids participating in a Poli Obs was learning how to negotiate with their teachers regarding the handling of missed classes. The very fact that students not only asked permission of teachers to go on a Poli Obs, but learned how to discuss with the teachers their concerns, helped reduce resistance on the part of many teachers to students going on a Poli Obs. Some kids discovered that it was best for them not to miss a given class but instead work their Poli Obs time around the class. This was easiest if the class was first or second period in the morning, of course. But the key point is that, like the SEDS students at Northport, the Poli Obs students were learning adult, non-confrontational ways of handling conflicts.

As time went on, more and more kids started taking advantage of Poli Obs. By the end of the first year, about a fourth of my students had gone on at least one Poli Obs and quite a few went on more than one. Over the next few years that number increased to over half of my students. As the reputation of the program grew, other social studies teachers began using Poli Obs with their students.

The numbers are not as important as the fact that most kids gained something both in terms of substantive information and as an experience in self-direction. It was always a joy when students came in after going on a Poli Obs and excitedly described how things went. Most of the time, students were pleased and felt it was a worthwhile experience. Kids usually felt this way even when it was unsuccessful in terms of the substantive purpose, as when Peter, quoted in chapter 2, said ". . . going to the Supreme Court (on a Poli Obs) was a terrible experience . . . because we had no idea what we were doing, but . . . I learned that I would do it better next time."

SEDS was remedial

Bruce Hunt says that, wonderful as SEDS was, it was remedial! He is right, of course. The SEDS concept of encouraging kids to do and think for themselves, and to take charge of their own learning, should be the central core of the school experience, not a side program to be participated in by a handful of kids willing to take risks or clever enough to see its possibilities for learning and for coping with the system.

In a sense, Poli Obs was also remedial, although it was a step beyond SEDS because it was incorporated into the regular school program. But it too was an add-on. Students had to make special arrangements to participate. And while that provided an opportunity for students to learn such adult skills as negotiating for time and space to do what they wanted, it remains that Poli Obs and SEDS are half-way houses at best: opportunities for some kids to sneak experiences in self-direction and independent learning into a generally other-directed and boring school day.

That Curry and I were successful in keeping a program like Poli Obs in a public high school was no accident. We worked at keeping the program low-key and out of the limelight. Unlike with SEDS, there were no daily lists of students going on a Poli Obs. Each student had to secure teacher permission individually. We deliberately kept control of the records—students had to return both teacher and parent forms to us, not to a secretary, and each day that we had any students on a Poli Obs we would simply turn in the list of their names so they would be included on the daily absence lists as being "excused." But lurking in the background was considerable anxiety among many teachers and parents that this program would lead to the students going wild and getting in trouble. There is great resistance in schools to making involving, self-directed experiences for students the norm rather than the exception.

The psychologist Erik Erikson has provided a clue as to why this is so. In *Childhood and Society*[4], Erikson analyzes an unusual baby-swaddling pattern among Russian peasants. The custom among these people was to swaddle infants for their first nine months of life "up to the neck, tightly enough to make a handy 'log of wood' out of the whole bundle . . . for the greater part of the day and throughout the night."[5] When asked why they had this custom, the Russians answered that there is no other way to keep babies warm through a Russian winter and, "besides, how could one otherwise keep [a baby] from scratching and harming himself, and of scaring himself with the sight of his own hands?"[6]

Erikson analyzes this as follows: "Now it is probably true that a swaddled baby, especially when just unswaddled, has not sufficient mastery over his own movements to keep from scratching and hitting himself. The further assumption that *therefore* he has to be swaddled again is a favorite trick of cultural rationalization [Erikson's emphasis]. It makes a particular pattern of infant-restraint culturally self-supporting. You must swaddle the infant to protect him against himself; this causes violent vasomotor needs in him; he must remain emotionally swaddled in order not to fall victim to wild emotion. This, in turn, helps to establish a basic, a proverbial, indoctrination, according to which people, for their own good, must be rigidly restrained while being offered, now and then, ways of discharging compressed emotion."[7] Erikson's analysis of the Russian baby-swaddling is almost deliciously applicable to the general pattern of infantilizing students in American public high schools. Many teachers (and other people) find the idea of kids' being meaningfully involved in their own learning, and being self-directed, as threatening. The passive mode of most school learning is safer for teachers because they can more easily set limits and control the kids. Many fear that if kids truly are involved and self-directed, they will ask difficult questions and will want to go beyond the limits now generally set for them. The fears are justified: kids will and should want to go beyond the limits of other-directed education. Thus, to justify these fears many adults say that kids cannot be allowed to be self-directed and independent because they will goof off, get in trouble, not do what they are "supposed" to do. So, they are seldom given a chance to learn how to be self-directed. And, when they are given a chance now and then, they sometimes *do* goof off. Thus, there exists a "culturally self-supporting [pattern]," in Erikson's phrase.

Students are not only infantilized by being directed in most of their school activities, but by being given little genuine choice about what or when or how they learn, and by being denied meaningful opportunities to learn to be self-directed and independent. They are also infantilized by being kept in the dark about how things run in the world. Yes, they can get some glimpse of this from television, though a rather distorted glimpse. And some kids come from families that teach them about the social/ political world of which they are a part. But the vast majority of students are appallingly ignorant of the world around them. They are puzzled and confused because have been kept in the dark most of their lives. Students generally are even ignorant about the one institution (other than their family) that affects them most directly: the school system. Kids have virtually no idea how schools are run or who makes decisions. One consequence of this is that when they have concerns or questions having to do with their own courses of study or school experiences, they do not know who to ask or how to go about finding out information—or how to effectively appeal or protest decisions.

A major part of encouraging students' curiosity is to help them lift this veil of mystery that frequently surrounds familiar institutions. If people understand how an institution such as the school system works, they can see how it affects them and how they can affect it. Part of this process entails helping students learn how to clearly observe the institutions and individuals that affect them (schools, legislatures, political leaders, and so forth) and how to accurately assess what they see. Students need to be strongly encouraged to intelligently question their own assumptions as well as to intelligently question the rhetoric of political leaders, from school principals and superintendents to U.S. Presidents. Assignments and activities that require students to question, to assess data, to develop supportable conclusions—all this should be the norm of formal education, not a side show that comes after students are forced to memorize material to be spit back on tests.

It's not that students are uninterested. On the contrary, most are very interested in what's going on in the larger world around them. They *do* want to know; they *are* curious. But they so often feel that what they think and want to know about is unimportant, is not what the system wants them to know, that they simply turn off. Yet, when they are encouraged to find out about their world, to ask questions, to become informed, most students readily do so. It is fascinating to watch kids became interested in how the school system runs and who has power in it, once they start to learn about it. One can almost see the lights go on in their heads. This applies to most subjects that they had heard about but had little comprehension of. Suddenly, students come alive with questions and relevant comments: "So that's what the school superintendent does?" Or, "that's why you always hear about how the stock market is doing on the news." Or, "I actually watched the news last night and understood most of it."

Helping students lift the veil of mystery about their institutions and their world does not require gimmicks or massive outlays of money. It requires an environment that encourages students to learn how to find out about things and a commitment by teachers to actively help them in this process. For example, on the wall in my classroom was a question I referred to frequently: "Who Decides, Who Benefits?" I was urging the students to always ask this question when analyzing all political actions, whether in the national government or in a school or wherever. Hence, a primary goal should be to strongly encourage students to become self-directed—to become self-actualized, in A.H. Maslow's phrase. Self-directed, self-actualized people are curious about the world around them. They participate actively, not passively, in life. They are much more likely to be the kind of intelligent citizens necessary to the functioning, indeed to the survival, of our democracy. There is a close link between encouraging students' curiosity about the world and their roles in it, and helping them become self-directed, self-actualized, independent adults.

Does it work? Will students in fact respond to an environment that encourages their curiosity about their world, encourages them to get involved in the world, and treats them in an adult manner and does not infantilize them? Will they buy into their own learning? Will they at least move toward becoming self-directed? Of course they will. Here is some evidence gathered from students' evaluations of 1988 and 1990 government courses:

> I learned so much about myself and how I think. I feel I owe you so very much for what you have given me and what you have taught me. The calm manner in the classroom and the maturity with which you treated us has spoiled me for other teachers. The bottom lines you continually stressed [no simple answers, many sides to every issue, Who decides/Who benefits] were *painful* yet *invaluable*. Thank you so very much. [student's emphasis]

> I feel that I have learned many new insights on ideas and concepts in the world we live in. We are learning to put ourselves in the situation of being an adult. I believe that your goal was more along the lines of trying to make us see who we are in relation to the world.

> This year I have learned many things, but most importantly that I need to *get involved*. [student's emphasis] This is the single most important thing which will affect my life both now & later. The environment of the room has definitely helped, because it directs the discussion to the students and not only to the teacher . . . it was both fun & interesting because I was involved, which helped me to understand not just memorize . . . [to] learn . . . about not only our government, but our society and how it works.

Jeff Mitroff said he would have gained more from the class environment had it been introduced earlier in his school life:

> I think the environment helped me learn as best I could with it. Meaning, if I had been exposed to this earlier than I would have learned a lot more than in any traditional classroom. As it was this year, I think because it was a new experience I learned about the same. More importantly, this classroom got me ready for college: to not count on the teacher to have me learn but, to quote a famous philosopher (smile), "buy into it" myself. For this I thank you. I only wish this approach had been used earlier.

The sentiments of these recent high school graduates also were expressed in a June 1971 audio-taped conversation by some senior students at Yellow Springs High School (different ones from those quoted in an earlier chapter). I asked them what they thought were their most useful experiences during their high school careers—"not necessarily things you liked most but what you think are/will be most useful to you." This is part of the response:

Nina: I think maybe your class was. Why? Because we are doing things for ourselves rather than always being told what to do.

Lil: I think the New York trip put it all in focus because . . . a lot of things we learned in class about interest groups you could see in that city . . . and being able to take care of yourself, do things on your own in The Big City.

Thad: [I feel the] same as Nina, re: learning because I am involved, doing things on own.

Dora: I have learned more this year than the past three years. I think it is because I have had more freedom . . .

A big impediment to creating a school environment in which students are not infantilized is the difficulty adults have in understanding and coping with adolescence. Kids have a hard time coping with adolescence, too.

During adolescence young people begin more than ever to establish their sexual identities and start to develop relations with members of the opposite sex. Because in modern American society the school is the central meeting place for youth it is often less important as a place to learn information than as a place to develop socially.

Kids are highly aware of this, of course. Yes, in their different ways they want to develop intellectually. But what grabs them emotionally is their social development and especially their developing sexuality. One can chart this on a continuum line from those adolescents for whom the issue of sexuality is a blatantly overwhelming fact of their lives to those for whom it is something always lurking in the background. But no matter where an adolescent is along this continuum, the issue of sexuality is *always* there. And for good reason. The physical facts of puberty and sexual development and interest, along with the ways these facts are dealt with in our society, are a major part of the daily lives of young people, whether they are actively involved socially and sexually (the blatant group) or have few friends (the lurking group) or anywhere in between these extremes. Absolutely no subject can bring kids to attention faster. None. And in classes where they feel bored or uninvolved, thinking about sex is an escape hatch for them. And for the teacher who senses their boredom, raising the subject is a way to wake the kids up. As Clancy said during an audio-taped conversation in May 1990:

If you got an engaging teacher . . . that really holds your interest, ok . . . [but] if you got a teacher [who is] boring . . . you usually start doodling, drawing a picture of what you think his wife might look like . . . but then he starts talking about, ". . . did you know the fall of Rome was tied to their large use of concubines, and . . . when they made this, you know, temple of whores, they used it . . .," it's like, "Wow, really? I'll learn that!" You know, it really kind of helps to . . . bring up sex.

We live in an age when discussion about sexuality is much more open then ever. And, if we are to believe what kids tell us, a far higher percent of adolescents are sexually active than ever. And yet, with all this—a century after Freud brought sex out of the closet and half a century after Kinsey pulled it to the center of the living room for discussion—there still are vast numbers of adults, including most teachers, who are afraid to talk with kids honestly about sex. This is a serious problem, and very much relates to the tendency to infantilize them. It also relates to the on-going conflicts with kids over doing school work, attending classes regularly and paying attention to the teacher. When adults ignore the pre-eminent fact for high school kids of social development in general and dealing with their sexuality in particular, they significantly undermine the possibility of getting kids to voluntarily take seriously the need to also develop their intellects.

I am not saying that adults should become obsessed by sex. But honest, open adult acknowledgement of the importance of the issue for young people must be incorporated into adult dealing with kids. There are serious, legitimate concerns about young people not being able to handle, emotionally or financially, the consequences of sexual activity. Kids themselves are very concerned. They are very aware of and concerned about such matters as adolescent pregnancy and AIDS. But they often do not know how to mesh this awareness and concern with their normal sexual desires and with their normal desire to develop socially, let alone how to do this in ways that are comfortable for them and also psychologically and physically healthy. So when 13–19 year old people, struggling with all this without much adult empathy, having their feelings and fears discounted, are told they must do boring and apparently not-very-useful school work, they get angry and frustrated. They often rebel in ways that seem inappropriate and self-defeating.

Though adolescence has always been a turbulent time, it has become more difficult and more complicated in the past forty years. This is partly because the conflict between being biologically adult and mentally young has been increased by the affluence and technology of the second half of

this century. And it is partly because adolescence has been crassly trans-
formed from a time period between childhood and adulthood into a
commercial market—the teenage years.

With all the greater openness about sexuality in our time, the conflicts around it are also greater. For at the same time there has developed
greater openness about sexuality there also has developed greater pressure
on young people to delay adulthood. The very fact of the increased material affluence of most Americans since 1945 means there is increased pressure on kids to stay in school longer and to get good grades in order to
be able to take advantage of the good life. So more people delay assuming
the traditional adult responsibilities of marriage, family, home. That this
also means greater opportunities for economic and personal development
does not alter the fact that the biological urges are still strong. An adolescent boy or girl looking ahead to adulthood sees a very long road and,
in effect, is likely to feel no point in waiting to be sexually active—especially since protection against pregnancy, the greatest fear prior to the
emergence of AIDS, is so easy to obtain.

In short, it is not only very difficult to be an adolescent today, it is
very difficult to leave adolescence and become an adult. High schools
greatly exacerbate the problem when they infantilize kids by not providing
opportunities for them to learn and grow and move more effectively into
adulthood.

It is fascinating to see the differences in behavior of students on
their after school jobs and during school. A high percentage of high school
kids have jobs during the school year. These often are quite responsible
jobs—store clerk, waiter or waitress, an aide in a day-care center, deliv-
ering food, office work. At their jobs they are mature, serious, at ease
with themselves, quite adult. At school they are different people, often
immature-acting, flighty, clearly uncomfortable—being silly in class,
being unwilling to participate in discussions or respond to reasonable questions, fooling around a lot. I see this as a response to the infantilizing
that they experience at school. If they can be mature and responsible on
jobs, why not in school?

The answer is simple: in general, schools neither encourage nor
allow students to function as they do on jobs. Nor do schools reward
students for adult behavior as jobs do, either financially or otherwise. To
the contrary, schools reward infantile, submissive behavior to keep the
kids in line.

Certainly not all young people can function independently at the
same level of effectiveness at the same age. Maturation and cognitive

skills do not develop at the same pace for everyone. But *most* students can function independently in different ways and at different points in their development. Schools should not hand students a line of baloney about the world or shield them from its realities. Schools *should* help students prepare to deal with those realities. Given genuine opportunities, being taken seriously and treated with respect by teachers and other adults, most students can and will learn to be independent, involved in their own learning, and self-directed.

Notes

1. Letter to author, December 11, 1990.
2. As an experiment that year, I had a class in government that was actually two class-sized groups assigned to me in one period. I met in a formal class session twice a week with each group. On the fifth day the kids worked individually and I met with individual kids or small groups, or sometimes we had a speaker or a film for both classes. On the whole the arrangement worked very well.
3. She refers to an unpopular assistant principal who *was* hostile to SEDS
4. W.W. Norton, 1950
5. 35th anniversary edition, 1985, p. 388
6. ibid
7. ibid, pp. 388–89

7

Teachers: How Do You Know a Good One if You See One?

T o be a good teacher is to hold, at the same time, one of the most difficult and the most satisfying jobs imaginable.

A good teacher is excited about learning and about helping students learn. A good teacher truly cares about the kids as people, genuinely reaches out to them, does not see them as the enemy, does not assume a confrontational stance with them—creates a we/we environment, not a we/they environment. A good teacher is always alert to the teachable moment—those times when, for example, a student suddenly asks a question or makes a point that may only be tangentially related to the matter at hand in the class but which triggers thoughts or insights in the teacher that provide golden opportunities to help students better understand something. Recognizing the teachable moment requires that teachers be flexible. They must not be so wedded to a lesson plan that they cannot take advantage of these unexpected opportunities. A good teacher does not routinely fall apart in the face of such trivia as students occasionally being late to class or missing class altogether or not having a pass when late but keeps her or his eye on the target of helping the students learn and grow. A good teacher encourages the students to work hard, to think, to question. A good teacher involves kids in the process of their own learning and helps them relate that learning to the rest of the world.

There's more. A good teacher is knowledgeable about the subject matter being taught, but keeps the value of that subject matter in perspective. That is, while being knowledgeable about the subject matter, even enthusiastic about it, a good teacher also knows that students have other subjects to learn and does not assign work and make demands that assume her or his subject is the only one the students have to deal with. Indeed, a good teacher knows that the subject-matter is rarely as important to the students as are other matters in their lives, and understands that for high school-age people there are necessary realities that consume their primary energies. Coping with growing up, developing their own values, relating to peers and adults, and checking out the world and its possibilities, all these compete with studying in students' lives. Thus, a good teacher exhibits this knowledge and understanding by trying to make the subject matter relate to the rest of their world. In fact, a good teacher understands that ultimately his or her primary job is to help kids find their own way.

Is all this possible? Of course. But it is not easy. It takes hard work and energy to develop and maintain relationships with young people and help them help themselves. But it is worthwhile and satisfying. The energy it takes to be a good teacher causes a relaxed tiredness at day's end—not the angry, exhausted tiredness many teachers frequently feel. Not only is being a good teacher rewarding, it is necessary if our goal is to help young people become enlightened, knowledgeable, questioning, self-directed adults.

Common threads

How do students know a good teacher when they see one? They do not all have the same perceptions. Different teacher characteristics are important for different students. Yet there are common threads that run through the various student perceptions of what makes a teacher seem to them good. Listen to what some former students say:

For George, a 1989 South Lakes graduate, good teachers were the ones who helped him with life skills and who truly cared about the kids:

> There are certain teachers whom I have a lot to thank for . . . They were the ones who gave me knowledge and skills which not only help [me] to exist in this society better, but which allow me to enjoy life more. There were very few teachers whom this can be said about, however, and all too many were only concerned with having the students parrot information back to them on worthless multiple choice or true-false tests. Having the students really learn anything was of only secondary concern, which was frequently justified by placing the blame on the students with the oft heard statement, "I can't *make* them learn anything!" They simply weren't interested in trying to teach in the first place. There was not a real sense of concern

for the student, whether he (she) really learned anything or not was of no consequence. Students sense this attitude in their instructors and often lose interest in the class and what the teacher has to say.

George was not the only one who felt a caring teacher was a good one. Here are comments from three students on their 1990 government course evaluations:

As a teacher . . . You acted human and showed compassion for your students and that is seriously lacking in . . . school.

I see now the importance of learning on your own without [teacher] threats. . . . [only] some teachers really give a damn.

This class has been excellent. The environment is more human. Instead of a teacher who is just rattling off assignments to us you talk to us. I would recommend this style of teaching around the country.

Jerome, South Lakes Class of 1988, said in a 1990 audio-taped interview that a good teacher takes an interest in students:

I guess I would have liked teachers who paid more attention to me . . . I know that's hard for them, but . . . when you are a teacher you have to believe, you have to have this egalitarian view that every kid is smart innately and you can't give up on any of them . . .

For some students, the important thing is for teachers to be excited about what they teach, to involve the kids in process of learning and to encourage kids to think and question:

In general, the most valuable experiences I had [in high school] were the teachers . . . [who] were excited about the subject being taught, which caused me to have more interest. [Sherry, South Lakes class of 1989, in her alumni survey]

The best learning situations for me were those in which teachers lectured informally and encouraged questions & class discussions. Especially helpful were teachers who facilitated this by mentioning various viewpoints and asking what students believed and why. In addition, teachers who made themselves approachable & displayed a sense of humor created a more comfortable learning environment. [Veronica, South Lakes class of 1987, in her alumni survey]

Kristen Burke, a 1987 South Lakes graduate, sent me in 1990 a copy of a short essay she wrote for a college class in 1989. It expresses Kristen's perception of what makes a teacher good, as well as being flattering to me. Like others, she thinks a good teacher is one who is excited about what he or she is doing, involves kids in the process, and helps kids think:

> . . . Mr. Tripp['s] . . . greatest quality was his enthusiasm. The class was caught up in his excitement to learn. This excitement motivated me to push myself to understand and eventually really learn the material . . . [he] really loved the whole concept of learning. He hated when his classes were interrupted by the P.A. system, pep rallies, or other trivial events. He really wanted us to learn as much as he could teach us in what little time he had . . . [an] equally important quality was his style of questioning. He would phrase his questions so they were on a higher level than simple knowledge and comprehension. We were taught to apply our previous knowledge, to analyze situations, and to evaluate rules and laws of society. [He] would push us to think harder, especially if he knew we weren't really using our minds to full capability.

During a 1990 audio-taped discussion, Mary and Henry, two South Lakes seniors, said that a good teacher pushes kids to think, to work harder and to relate what they learn to the rest of the world:

Mary: Well, the good ones are when a teacher will pressure you . . . so that you will work yourself harder and you'll push yourself harder. But not uncaring [teachers] . . .

Henry: As she says, the [good teachers are] ones that make you think and want to make you work hard. Probably the most important are the ones that are more [related] to what's going to happen in your life, [who] give assignments that deal with real life instead of just sort of busywork to keep you busy, stuff that you'll forget, [who give] actual stuff that you can go out into the world and use, are the ones that I'll remember.

So why aren't there more good teachers? Is it simply because it is too hard and that for many teachers the rewards do not compensate for the difficulties?

Infantilizing teachers

Too many teachers allow themselves to be infantilized, much as the school infantilizes students. The condition of public school teaching militates against there being more good teachers. They are neither trained to become good teachers nor once on the job are they generally supported by the system to be good teachers.

In 1963 I attended a meeting of teachers from all over Long Island whose schools were hosting foreign students under the old New York

Herald-Tribune foreign student program. I came away thoroughly depressed after listening to the talk of fellow teachers before and after the meeting. Most of it was complaining that "they" hadn't yet given "us" the new curriculum guides we had been told about, so how could we prepare the kids for the Regents' exam? These were primarily social studies teachers, referring to New York State's end-of-school year state-wide exams in U.S. and world history.

This was depressing because it reflected a feeling of helplessness on the part of the teachers: they were not in charge of their own professional lives and felt they could not act on their own initiative. No wonder so many teachers are not happy and so many kids are bored out of their skulls.

The state did not prescribe a set curriculum, as such. It did offer a Regents' diploma which was more prestigious than a regular diploma and carried with it the possibility of college scholarship money. It was important for teachers to know generally what kinds of areas and issues the exam would deal with. But it was not necessary to follow a particular curriculum to prepare the students. There was a wide latitude for teachers to be creative. That is why the discussion at that meeting so depressing. The teachers felt they could not work out their own approach to preparing the students, but had to wait for the guidelines that came from the New York State Department of Education.

That is one way many teachers have become infantilized: instead of being encouraged to be creative and take charge of their work, they are encouraged to wait for someone else to tell them not only what to do but how to do it. Teachers easily become dependent on curriculum guides that spell out not only what is to be covered but how to cover it. And while it is perfectly reasonable for teachers to use or adapt suggestions from a curriculum guide, they should not be so wedded to these guides that they cannot or do not think for themselves and develop their own methods.

A major reason why many teachers are attached to directives from the state or from their school system is that it is safer to behave this way. If teachers follow curriculum guides or directives they run fewer risks of being challenged by a parent or administrator for teaching or using some "wrong" method. Moreover, for many teachers sticking closely to guides is simply easier. They don't have to think. They can develop neat formulas for teaching. Of course, this is also a formula for boring classes. But teachers who are wedded to guides seldom think about that.

Teaching tends to attract people who are not risk-takers. Historically, a strong appeal of teaching is that it is one of the safest, most secure jobs around. In general, the system does nothing to discourage this feeling. After all, it is much easier to control contented cows in the pasture than curious goats who explore the hillside on their own.

But while the system tends to infantilize teachers as it does students, teachers must bear much more responsibility for their own infantilization than do students. After all, they *are* adults. They like to think of themselves as professionals. Yet the comments I heard from so many teachers at that Long Island meeting 30 years ago showed not only the infantilization of teachers, but also showed the tendency of teachers to react to that condition by whining and moaning. I have seen very little change over the years.

Yet, having said this, it must also be said that the particular nature of public school teaching does create special if not unique circumstances. This is not an excuse, but at least some of the reason that teachers allow themselves to be infantilized—and so cannot function in adult, creative ways that more effectively help kids learn and grow.

Most people work hard at their jobs. They are tired when they come home. They have complaints. There are things at work that irritate them, that they are sure can be done better. They often feel they are not appreciated, or that undeserving people get promoted ahead of them. In this sense teachers are no different from the rest of the working population.

Life in a fishbowl

However, few if any occupations in this country operate in the public limelight as much as teaching does. Teachers live professionally in a glass fishbowl. Most people feel quite able and willing to tell the schools how to operate. We all went to school, didn't we? Schools are political footballs. Public discussion about education abounds. Politicians run for elected office partly on promises to do *something* about the schools. Of course, there is some legitimacy to all this, since our public schools *are* public, are for the most part run by elected school boards. But the classroom teacher remains in the glass fishbowl. And one consequence of this is that teachers feel particularly vulnerable and feel a particularly strong need to be understood.

It sometimes looks as if teachers don't work very hard, or anyway don't work very much. They come home at three or four in the afternoon, don't they? And they generally have longer vacations than most people— ten days at Christmas, a week's spring break, eight or nine weeks in the summer, in some places a week's mid-winter break in February, always a four-day weekend at Thanksgiving. But what many people forget is that for most teachers the workday does not end when they come home. There are always papers to check, tests to grade, lessons to prepare. Vacations are a time to catch up on correcting and planning as much as a time to rest. The summer is a time to take courses to update skills and knowledge required in most states for teachers to maintain their certification which is necessary to be employed in the public schools. Summer is also a time to do long-range planning and preparation of materials, and a time to develop curricula.

Moreover, teaching drains the teacher. No matter how much one may enjoy and love kids, working each day with 120 to 150 of them in a high school, or with 20 to 30 young ones in an elementary school, is a very tiring enterprise. Yes, it is generally rewarding, but it is also an energy drain. Believe me, one needs breaks from that. This is not a complaint. It is a fact of life that "comes with the territory."[1] So while it may appear that teachers don't work hard, or don't work long hours, it's not true. They work hard and work long hours. Teachers do need to be understood in terms of their own circumstances.

Yes, there are some high school teachers who get by with doing the minimum possible with students. As has been said, they have taught one year 25 times. They figured out how to do the job with a minimum of effort their first year in teaching and repeated the same thing for the rest of their career. They are the ones who not only do not work hard, they actively help make school a game.

But this dreary description fits a minority of teachers. Most teachers *do* work hard. They plan lessons and give and correct assignments such as tests and essays, usually spending hours at home each day and very often during much of the weekend. They monitor behavior and sign passes and check homework. Most high school teachers conduct five classes a day. They have telephone and face-to-face conferences with parents and counselors. They attend frequent faculty meetings. They have to do endless paperwork. The average high school teacher has several thousand interactions a day with students, colleagues, and others. That takes a great deal of energy.

What makes this energy drain especially sad is that much of it is not the result of actually working with young people. The drain is probably greater with teachers who create a we/they environment and pit themselves against the kids and noticeably less with teachers who create a we/we environment. But for all teachers, the extraordinary energy drain results from a combination of negative factors. Teachers have to comply with stupid bureaucratic rules. They must spend time and energy keeping uncomprehending critics at bay, such as punitive administrators. Hostile parents sometimes expect the school to do for their children what they, themselves, do not or cannot do. Of course, if teachers were better trained to work with parents and to deal more effectively with their anger, and if the system supported teachers in such efforts, then the whole matter of hostile parents would be vastly different and much less of a problem. And it would be a lighter drain of energy.

Teaching teachers

Teacher training is another problem. Most people who go through teacher training programs find that much of it is not very helpful. This could be the subject of a whole book in itself. It will be discussed only briefly here.

There is a lack of congruence between teacher training and the experience teachers find in schools. Part of this is because up to date teacher training programs inform prospective teachers about techniques that schools have not yet adopted. Consequently, the teachers may not be able to put these new techniques into practice. Training programs also sometimes introduce a more enlightened version of the teaching-learning process than exists in public schools.

Of course prospective teachers should be exposed to good techniques and enlightened views. But they also need to understand the difference between the training program and reality. And they need to see how they can create for themselves ways of rising above the banality of most schools. If teacher training included self-awareness experiences, it might provide prospective teachers with some psychological tools necessary to deal with the system. Then they would be less likely to be taken in or dragged down by it. Instead, the training high school teachers receive includes very little about adolescent behavior, let alone about teacher behavior in general. It seldom touches on the need to know oneself well if one is to work effectively and non-confrontationally with students.

Part of this is because most teacher training programs are part of the same system as the schools. The training colleges have a big stake in things as they are. A kind of old-boy network develops between teacher training colleges and the schools. Generally, prospective teachers are not encouraged to challenge the schools' premises or the we/they atmosphere that is the norm. The net result is that most people complete teacher training with a minimum of knowledge about themselves and how to realistically cope with the schools. They have not learned how to effectively challenge faulty premises of how learning takes place. They don't know how to challenge the confrontational, often destructive practices they may encounter in schools.

Once on the job, neophyte teachers find it easier and safer to follow the formal and informal rules of the system. They fall into the clutches of experienced teachers who often are very cynical about kids, learning, new ideas—and teacher training colleges. "This is *the* way kids are and this is *the* way the system is and don't buck it, don't come up with all this new-fangled stuff," is a common line new teachers hear. They have to be unusually tough, secure and aware to withstand that. Often new teachers are pulled down to the level of the older ones because they cave in hoping to gain some status and favor—much the same way oppressed people sometimes deal with their oppressors. And then the older teachers' behavior becomes a habit with the newer teachers until they, too, become cynical older teachers.

The occupational hazards of public school teaching will be less of a problem for teachers when public esteem for them and for serious learning is higher. That requires a serious national dialogue about the purpose of education and the role of the schools as an institution. When this takes place, there will be no questions of whether or not teachers work hard, or as hard as other folks. It will be understood that, like any job, teaching has its own set of frustrations and difficulties, just as it has its own particular joys and rewards.

What can teachers do?

Meanwhile, even with all the institutional constraints of the school system as it is, there things that teachers can do that would improve the general public view of them—and thus decrease the need to spend energy coping with negative public perceptions. There are things teachers can do to make their own lives more satisfying and at the same time do a better job of teaching. There are things teachers can do to take charge of their own professional lives in the same sense that students should be encouraged to take charge of their own learning. What are some of the things teachers can do?

They can change their teaching methods to encourage students to become excited about learning instead of being bored by it. Among other things, teachers can move away from busywork assignments that turn students off and toward more creative, long-range assignments. The *Merriam-Webster Dictionary's* definition of busywork is "work that appears productive but only keeps one occupied."[2] Typical of high school busywork is the textbook homework assignment: "Read chapter three and answer the questions at the end." Frequently kids get those kinds of homework assignments night after night. The next day, the teacher collects the homework, goes over it, and then lectures the kids about that night's assignment. Every so often the teacher gives the kids a test on the homework. Sometimes the teacher gives the students time in class to start the homework. This not only turns class time into a study hall, but reduces meaningful teacher involvement with the students.

Teachers who give nightly textbook homework assignments do not call them busywork, of course. They are trying to force students to study and learn. But that is not the result for most kids. Those who usually do the assignments do so not because they think they learn from them but because they accept that they must do them to get a good grade. Students who do not do such assignments, or only do them in a half-hearted way, are rebelling; for these kids, the lure of the grade is not great enough to overcome their rebellion. Al, a 1988 graduate of South Lakes High School, offered a common reaction to homework on his alumni survey:

> I never seemed to get past teachers who thought the best way to teach was to assign lots of "busywork." . . . Testing kids to see if they can remember a bunch of dates is pointless. Teachers ought to show students how to use what they learn, in the real world. Bring current events, modern literature, and science into the classroom. Show, don't tell.

Once in a while, overnight homework assignments no doubt are necessary. And, as long as the students understand their purpose and do not have them as a steady diet, they can be useful. But teachers are much more likely to excite students about learning if they use long-range assignments that challenge students to think, explore, question and reason. Here is an example of what I am talking about.

In my American government course one of my aims was to get the kids to understand and grapple with the issues in our society that government deals with. One issue is racial discrimination, and its underlying premise of racism. To help the students start to understand and grapple with this issue, they were assigned to read Martin Luther King's *Letter from a Birmingham Jail*,[3] written in 1963, and Chief Justice Earl Warren's opinion in the landmark 1954 Supreme Court decision in *Brown v. the Board of Education*.[4] The students were to write a three–five page essay analyzing the two items, discussing their relationship to each other and their meaning today. They had several weeks to complete the assignment. Prior to receiving the assignment the students had begun to learn about racism and discrimination, and about the governmental and societal structures and political practices that institutionalize discrimination. The assignment also helped students learn about political strategies necessary to change laws and practices.

The essays were critiqued and returned to the students. This presented yet another opportunity to discuss issues and related information. Constructive feedback is part of the dialogue and relationship that should exist between teachers and students.

A variation of the King *Letter*/Warren opinion assignment was used in an advanced, two-credit 9th grade course in world civilization that I taught at South Lakes High School with Pam Curtis, an English teacher. The students were told to read King's *Letter from a Birmingham Jail* in conjunction with reading Sophocles' *Antigone*. Here the aim was to help the students see that *Antigone*'s tragedy involved civil disobedience, and that this has a modern dimension. This not only helped the students see that *Antigone* has a powerful meaning for our time but also used the play and King's *Letter* to open discussion of issues of racism and discrimination.

Not every assignment in every course can be crafted the same way as these uses of King's *Letter*. Nor would such an approach always be appropriate. But an approach that requires students to reason and make connections among relevant facts and concepts should be the norm of school lessons, not the exception.

There are, of course, other ways available to a good teacher to involve kids and get them to learn concepts and ideas along with basic information. Simulations, role-playing and field trips can be applied in a variety of academic situations. In simulations, students re-create in the classroom real-life situations—such as a session of a legislature or an historical event or people visiting a foreign country and having to use a foreign langue—to give them a feel for reality. A science lab is a simulation by another name. Role-playing is a cousin of simulation exercises but typically involves only a few people at a time responding in a particular role to some crisis or problem; other members of the group watch the role-play and later join in analyzing what happened. Sometimes teachers and students see these kinds of activities as just fun and games. But, planned and executed carefully, they are excellent teaching tools that involve students in the learning process and require them to learn *in a context that gives the information meaning.*

Here is what two students said on their 1990 government course evaluations about the value of involving activities in contrast to the usual kinds of school work:

> What have I learned? Hmm. In a nutshell I have learned how our government and society work, including all the specifics (terms, procedures, etc.) Most beneficial have been the hands on experiences (field trips, simulations, etc.). For some reason these events stand out and are easy to remember. Also seeing government in action conveys a sense of action/tension beyond the stale SOS (Same Old Sh . . .) textbook. Specifically, my trips to Capitol Hill were the most influential: sitting there while men make decisions that affect our lives is exciting. At times I wanted to speak out. Anyway, this year has sparked a thirst for more knowledge and information that will help me better understand what's happening around me.

> The classroom environment has been superb! . . . the students are so incredibly informed and involved and we are dying of thirst for knowledge. I have become politically aware, and more interested.

Practising non-confrontation

Even within the limits of schools as they are, teachers can make it a practice to be non-confrontational with students. This is an integral part of maintaining a we/we classroom environment. Even in a classroom of 17–18 year old high school seniors, it is primarily up to teachers to set the tone, to create the atmosphere, to understand what is happening when a student becomes disruptive or angry or intransigent. Teachers are paid to do a job. Students are there involuntarily. Teachers do not have to bite when students challenge. Teachers can respond in non-hostile, non-confrontational ways. This is much easier if the teacher starts by believing, not that the kids are the enemy, but that teachers are there to help the kids learn, and that kids should be invited, not disinvited, into their classes.

I am not saying that if Henry tells Mr. Alverez to go to hell, or gives him the finger, Mr. Alverez should smile, pat Henry on the back, and say, "how cute." But Mr. Alverez does not have to instantly fall apart, hit the roof, order the kid to go to the office, and in other ways overreact self-righteously. Depending on the exact circumstances (Is this the first time Henry ever did that? How well does Mr. Alverez know Henry?) Mr. Alverez can use a variation of the "I Message" approach developed by Dr. Thomas Gordon in *T.E.T.: Teacher Effectiveness Training*[5] "I don't like you to say (or do) that; please don't. Now, can we talk about what the problem is?" And, again depending on the situation (during a class period, or at the end, or whatever), Mr. Alverez can arrange to talk with Henry then or later. In other words, Mr. Alverez can assume that an outburst like Henry's reflects something to be worked out, and is not merely an unnecessary assault on him.

Many teachers will say that is fine in theory but it doesn't work in reality. But, it does work 99% of the time. And teachers do not have to be super-human. What they do have to do is avoid letting a situation get to the point where only becoming Authower can end the difficulty. And this becomes not merely possible but likely in a we/we, non-confrontational environment. It is encouraged when the teacher assumes that the kids and she or he are in the same boat, seeking the same end. The teacher needs to demonstrate that his or her role and position are different from the students' only because of age, experience and, sometimes, accumulated wisdom. Even the wisest and most non-confrontational teacher sometimes get trapped into becoming Authower. But such times should be the exception, not the rule. The normal behaviors of teachers should not be based on the exceptions to the rule. The overwhelming majority of the time interactions with students can easily be pleasant and non-confrontational. If teachers and administrators create at the outset a we/we, inviting environment this will be even more certain.

To those who say that this approach either doesn't work or is "giving in" to the kids, as some teachers and administrators do say, the wisdom of the 4th Century Roman Emperor Julian provides guidance. While Julian was Caesar in Gaul, according to Edward Gibbon's account in *The Decline and Fall of the Roman Empire*,[6] Julian's general view of being in charge, whether of his soldiers in battle or of his subjects in civil matters, was as much as possible to suffer or exalt as they did and understand their situation as much as he could. In line with that philosophy, on one occasion Julian overruled one of his own advocates who had vigorously prosecuted a local official. "Who will ever be found guilty if it be enough to deny?" asked the prosecutor. And Julian replied, according to Gibbon: "And who will ever be innocent, if it is sufficient to affirm?" I'm with Julian. He understood a we/we, non-confrontational environment a long time ago.

But as things stand today near the end of the 20th century, the system does make it difficult to be a good teacher. It takes people who can get beyond infantilization, who can get beyond the general conditions of teaching and inadequate training.

It does not have to be this way. Training programs can prepare prospective teachers to be tough, self-aware, and aware of how the system operates and how one might function creatively and successfully within the system. And the schools themselves could encourage teachers to take the risks necessary to be intellectually and personally challenging educators who engage students to think, learn, grow and become self-directed adults.

This is not an easy task—and will not take place without much wrenching and many institutional changes. And there will be much resistance to change, of course. But movement for change can begin immediately, even on the smallest individual level. Indeed, it has begun on that level, among some teachers. As with defining good education, we need a serious, ongoing dialogue about the characteristics necessary to be good teachers.

One thing that will *not* help is multiple choice/essay tests which more and more states are requiring teachers to pass to become certified to teach. The ability to pass such a test in no way describes whether the person is able or willing to be the kind of creative, alive teacher we so desperately need in American schools. The pitfalls of basing judgements on paper-and-pencil tests described in chapter 11 applies as much to teachers as to students. We must devise much more sophisticated, sensitive ways of evaluating teachers—and take the risk of doing most of that evaluating once the teacher is actually working. As with preparing to be a parent, preparing to be a teacher can be done most effectively on the job with on-going support and guidance from exprienced people.

A side-effect of exciting kids to want to learn is that the public, especially the parents, feels much more positive about the teacher and more willing to understand the particular problems of teachers. Unfortunately, too many teachers do not excite kids, do not inspire kids to want to learn more and grow. Students who go home and complain about stupid, boring teachers do not encourage parents—the most visible part of the public for teachers—to think highly of teachers, to be understanding of their particular problems.

The irony, then, is that good teaching and learning is satisfying hard work that will significantly decrease the need to cope with negative public views of teachers. Certainly this was my experience. There is a close link between self-rewarding hard work, exciting kids to want to learn more, and parental (read: public) support.

So, how do you know a good teacher if you see one? Let the last word go to two former students:

> Even though I know you sometimes hate the school system, I've always known that you love to interact with and teach teenagers. *That* should be a prerequisite for a teacher!! [from a 1990 government course evaluation]

> The teachers are in two different groups: the motivated and the unmotivated. The motivated were the best teachers. They always seemed to care about not only the material but also the student's input . . . The motivated teachers also had more discussion in class. Students were not afraid to ask questions or make insightful points . . . On the other hand were the unmotivated teachers. These were the teachers who taught the necessary material, but would refuse to stray off the beaten trail. They would assume some questions [were] redundant when it was possible that other students have been thinking the same questions. Consequently, the students and the teacher are on two different wave-lengths. [Dan, a 1988 South Lakes graduate, in his alumni survey]

Notes

1. Charley, in Arthur Miller's *Death of a Salesman*, 1949; Viking Press edition, 1958, p. 138
2. Pocket Books, 1974, Page 106
3. Issued as a pamphlet by the American Friends Service Committee, May 1963
4. 374 US 483, May 1954
5. Peter Wyden, Publisher, 1974
6. Porter & Coats, 1845 edition, Volume II, p. 155

The Playing Field

8

The Institution: Sorting and Ranking

The blunt truth is that the institution of the high school serves only part of its target population very well—and then mainly as a conduit for society to move that population on to college and good jobs. The institution does not do what it should to help *all* young people learn and grow. The essential reason is that the avowed purpose of the school is undermined by a hidden agenda.

What are schools for?

The stated purpose of schools is to educate students. An unstated purpose is to provide a sorting out/ranking process whereby some students acquire the skills and information necessary to go on to college and high status careers while other students get by with whatever they can take from their school experience. Some students in this latter group do manage to gain some useful skills and knowledge but many others are lost along the way: they either drop out before graduating from high school or graduate with skills and knowledge inadequate to help them compete effectively for college places, jobs and advancement.[1]

This use of schools by society is not limited to this country. It is more obvious in Great Britain and many other European countries. But this does not mean that the sorting out/ranking does not go on in the United States. It merely means that the process is more subtle here. Schools are very good at covering up their sins and putting on a show—of giving the appearance of fulfilling their stated purpose and of being democratic and open equally to all students in the process, which is consistent with the image of schools most Americans have.

In most high schools students are encouraged to become involved in clubs and sports—so-called extra-curricular activities. Since most of these activities are open to all students without regard to their academic ability, they are "democratic." And most courses are open to most students—theoretically. But in fact the sorting out/ranking process goes on behind the scenes in a variety of ways. What appears to be an institution open to all students equally is in fact an institution that sorts and ranks them very effectively.

Athletics vs. academics

For one thing, students from the same socio-economic backgrounds tend to participate in the same activities. Partly, this is a reflection of what happens in the larger society. But the school does little to mitigate this phenomenon. Yes, in recent years high schools have encouraged minority students (African-American, Hispanic, Asian) to join clubs they otherwise might not participate in. Yet school-related organizations still tend to be segregated by class and race. While it is no longer uncommon to see a black cheerleader, the overwhelming majority of cheerleaders is still white, petite, and "cute" in the television ad sense. Though in suburban high schools with a minority black population there are white kids on the football and basketball teams, is it an accident that a disproportionately high percent of these teams is composed of black kids? Or that, at the same time, the soccer, lacrosse and baseball teams are overwhelmingly white?

True, football and basketball teams have high status, so the black kids on these teams achieve a measure of success just being on them. In and of itself there is nothing wrong with that kind of success. The problem is that the success most of these kids experience in school is limited to sports. Indeed, probably to no other part of the school population does the institution do more of an injustice than to African-American athletes.

Some are very good academic students, but many are poor students who resist improving themselves scholastically. By no means are these stupid kids. They are intelligent and generally quite capable of doing academic work. But for most of them their school academic experiences are lousy. Many of these kids see themselves as incapable of doing well academically. Their way of dealing with these feelings is often to discount the value of academic pursuit, rationalizing that they are going to become professional athletes and do not need the academics.

But this is a terrible delusion that the institution perpetuates. Only a tiny fraction of high school athletes are successful professionally. They very much need to develop the skills and knowledge necessary to function effectively once they are out of school—whether in college or on a job. This is true for all kids, but it is especially true for black kids who must not only face competition from better prepared students but must face a racist society that will make it hard for them to succeed even when they have the requisite skills and knowledge.

I most emphatically am *not* saying that black kids should not play on high school sports teams. I *am* saying that they are being done a disservice by not being more actively helped to see the importance *for themselves* of pursuing academic as well as athletic goals. Generally, black athletes are not as strongly encouraged to do well academically as they are athletically. Had they been, then a far higher percent of them would be academically successful.

Hardy, a basketball star, was a classic non-achieving student: he frequently goofed off in class (when he bothered to come to class), and rarely did his assigned work. The sad fact was that Hardy could barely read at all, let alone at the level expected of a high school student. He saw school mainly as a way to meet friends and as an avenue to play professional basketball. It took much cajoling to get him to settle down enough to do *some* work and get at least a little involved in the course. Eventually, he hesitantly acknowledged that he needed to develop skills and knowledge other than basketball in case he did not succeed as a professional player. But he strongly resisted doing anything about developing those other skills.

Hardy's case is in no way unique. He was a nice young man for whom school had been a continuous disaster zone. He had received the message from very early on that he just didn't measure up. When he *was* academically encouraged by the institution it was mainly to get him to pass courses *in order to be eligible to play basketball*, since the school, as with most schools and athletic leagues, requires a minimum academic performance for students to play school sports. Hardy and others like him were generally not encouraged to do well academically in order to grow intellectually or to develop interests and talents other than athletics. Yet black kids have the same potential range of interests and abilities as any other population of students. What is different about black kids is that, by and large, they have not received from the school the same quality or quantity of academic encouragement as have white kids. To believe otherwise is to believe black kids are incapable of doing better academically. This is not true.

This situation is not the fault of the schools alone. There are social and economic factors that partly explain the frequently poor academic achievement of black kids. But while these factors may make more difficult the task of helping black kids achieve academically, they do not tip the balance. For the most part the school—the institution, the system—is an all-too-willing accomplice in the process.

The appeal of big-time sports is great for all young athletes, especially for young men. The salaries of the major sports' superstars shine like a beacon to young people—especially those from poor families. Athletics are glorified on television, in movies and in stories. And the institution lends a willing hand.

In fact, athletes are exploited by schools. Their athletic skills bring a kind of glory and prestige to the school that is reinforced by society in general. And the athletes are co-opted with sports rallies, banners in school urging the team to win and urging the student body to support the players, and cheerleaders cheering them on. Where in school can a young man or woman get this kind of recognition by doing well academically?

Another thing that supports the encouragement of black kids to stress athletics in high schools is the existence of college athletic scholarships. The argument is that if it were not for athletic scholarships, many black students could not afford college. But why is this so? Why don't the same proportion of black students as white students get academic scholarships? Do black kids have any less inherent ability than anyone else to earn the grades necessary for winning academic scholarships? Not if the institution gave them the same encouragement and support—the same education, if you will—as is given white kids.[2]

It is true that some black kids who go to college on athletic scholarships in fact do well academically. For one thing, not all black kids who get athletic scholarships were poor academic students in high school. But many were, *because their athletic abilities were encouraged in high school more than their academic abilities.* For another thing, some kids from any background mature later than others and start to blossom intellectually in college. My experience with all students tells me, however, that most could have developed academically while still in high school had they been sufficiently encouraged and effectively helped by the institution.

I place such stress on what generally happens to black kids in the sorting out/ranking process because it is such a blatant example. But it is by no means the only one.

Race and advanced placement

As stated earlier, most high school courses *theoretically* are open to most students. It is true that no social class or race of students is barred from taking any courses. Not directly, that is. But by virtue of placement in the accelerated or enriched classes and programs in elementary school and junior high school (classes and programs for students deemed especially "smart"), there is a close correlation between race and social class and who is in the high school accelerated courses—such as the so-called gifted-and-talented classes (GT) or the advanced placement classes (AP) or honors classes, as they are variously called. And it is from these kinds of classes that a high percentage of all kids going on to college come. In content and prestige, these courses are considered by the institution and by most students and parents to be the more desirable ones for college-bound kids.

For instance, during the two years I co-taught the 9th grade, GT world civilization course referred to in the previous chapter, we taught a total of 210 students over both years. The bulk of these students had been together in GT programs since elementary school. Over the two years there were 15 black students—or seven percent. At that time 13 percent of the school's students were black. There was also a disproportionately small percent of Asian and Hispanic students (two Asian, no Hispanic). It defies credulity that there were so few minority kids who could have been placed in the course.[3] To be sure, there are social and economic factors that were partly responsible for this situation. But the central point is that had there been strong, effective encouragement of minority kids to achieve academically throughout their school careers, there would naturally have been a much higher percent who entered the accelerated high school courses. As it is, then, these courses provide an effective way to sort out and rank students.

Nor is this only a sorting/ranking by race. Most of the majority white students in the world civ course had been in the GT track since elementary school and were students from higher socio-economic families. The institution would argue that the better academic students tend to come from these groups. Is this because these students are inherently superior academically to those from other social/racial classes? I doubt it. Or is it because the institution assumes they are, gives them preferential treatment, and moves them ahead on the accelerated tracks?

The sorting out/ranking is reinforced by the fact that students who tend to see each other all day long in the same classes also tend to be together in extra-curricular activities and in social events. The cumulative effect for the (mostly white) kids in the accelerated tracks is that they see themselves as successful, college bound, and assured of the good life (however each person interprets that). Many of the other kids see themselves as not particularly successful, bound for "inferior" colleges, if any college, and are less sure about their futures. The institution reinforces and helps to create the circumstances for this situation. Even in high schools where there is a relatively high percent of middle class black kids who are college bound, and college-bound white kids not in the accelerated tracks, the sorting out exists: in general, in courses and in activities, there is de facto if not de jure segregation by class and race.

Jason Kosnoski, a 1988 South Lakes graduate quoted earlier, has an insightful commentary on the sorting out/ranking process in high schools. This is his contribution to a 1990 audio-taped conversation about the social scene in high school:

> It was good in a sense . . . I learned to deal with people and deal with competition. But it was bad, [in that] it didn't mix [in] a lot of African American students . . . as I said [earlier] one of my best academic experiences was . . . your African Studies class, because I mixed with a lot of students I wouldn't have mixed with normally . . . I got to deal with people who were not white . . . middle class . . . because there were different socio-economic classes and backgrounds in . . . high school, but you never saw them mix, and I think that is also a function of the different tracks, you know, kids getting on the GT track, and kids getting on the remedial tracks and these kids never understand each other and that's where a lot of racism comes from—not necessarily overt racism . . . because you just don't deal with people like that [but] you reject things like their music and the way they talk and things like that as being stupid, when really it's just different.

Another perspective on the sorting out/ranking process is revealed by many of the students who were in the accelerated track since elementary school. These kids understand the sorting out process, and think they were lucky to be in the accelerated track where, they believe, they had the better teachers and were with the better students. Similar comments were repeated frequently.

Marty, a 1989 South Lakes graduate, is one of those who thought he was lucky to have been in the GT track because he felt he had the better teachers. His assessment of his high school experience on his alumni survey includes an analysis of the sorting out process and its consequences that is exceptionally interesting—and very damning:

I feel cheated. During my four years of high school I grew immensely, amazingly more than most probably; but when I think of how far I could have gotten in an ideal, well-structured environment, I feel sick. The gap between what I did achieve and what I could have achieved is astounding. Of the 24 teachers I had, I can only say that about four or five were of any real benefit to me. The rest of them [were] between mediocre and actually harmful to my growth as a human being. And I'm one of the lucky ones. Most of the "normal" or "average" people, who aren't in the Gifted classes that I was in, never come within a mile of really enlivening teaching. These days . . . in the public high schools, students who don't fit the established norms for intellectual value tend to fall by the wayside, so that the students who aren't particularly creative or curious . . . tend to get put in the more challenging classes because they are conformist, non-questioning, and good test-takers. These are the kids who get the good grades and test-scores that enable them to [use] the resources that could be more effectively used by those that are branded "underachievers," the artists and people with the curiosity, creativity and unwillingness to accept the situation as given them. In short, the qualities necessary for any serious intellectual pursuit. Public high schools give help to those that don't need it and discourage those that do. A natural-born conformist will get along no matter where he or she goes, because they do what ever the situation tells them to. But the people who work for more than the paltry opportunities the system gives them are going to have a much tougher time. They need the assistance and assurance from teachers at the high-school level that their modes of thought are just as legitimate as everyone else's. They also need the some opportunities to develop as people. The system needs to be made much more flexible before it will become adequate.

Race and societal values

Looked at another way, the institution—the system—separates all students, regardless of class and race, from the larger society. The institution serves as a holding pen for kids. For the most part it isolates young people from the rest of society so that it may carry out its function of imparting society's values to the young: such values as that all students should learn some basic knowledge and should be inculcated with the cultural norms; and that certain students should learn the skills and knowledge which will propel them to the top so that, when they become adults, they can carry on the society as is.

Some might ask, what is wrong with the institution having a sorting out/ranking function? Or, what is wrong with the institution's being a place whose purpose is to pass on the culture?

The answer is that the basis for the sorting and ranking is invalid. It is based primarily not on achievement or skill, but on social and economic class, and race. The chances of a student's acquiring the skills and knowledge necessary to function effectively in society, and to partake of the society's benefits, is immeasurably greater if that student is from the "right" class and race. As things now stand, the institution is a tool of society's dominant groups and values. That is not what an educational institution should be about.

Nor should an educational institution *unquestioningly* pass on the norms of society. Young people should learn not just the skills and knowledge society thinks they should know, but should also learn what they themselves see as important, and should learn to question and think independently. But that is a risky business. Allowing young people to think independently and to question means that the values of society may or may not get passed on intact. For some, that is a frightening thought. For me, it is an exciting thought. It is what school ought to be doing in the first place. Indeed, society is much more likely to be secure and usefully stable if in fact its young do learn to think independently and to question.

Of course, since the institution is supported by the dominant middle/upper middle class as a whole, it does generally reflect its values. But we really have never had a serious public dialogue about what we mean by good education. So there may not be a consensus even among the dominant groups about what they want for their schools. Those who run the schools (Authower) presume to know what these folks want and have managed to pacify and satisfy them enough to stave off much serious questioning—at least until fairly recently. And so long as middle/upper middle class people know how to work the institution enough to get for their kids the necessary skills and knowledge, the institution is not likely to change. Not unless its main clients can be shown what it is doing to its kids, and unless the economic and racial out groups develop the skills necessary to challenge the institution effectively.

Some are neglected

An interesting view of who does and does not benefit from the institution is provided by this excerpt from a May 1990 audio-taped conversation among three former South Lakes students. Elsie was in the 1990 graduating class. Alma and Jerome graduated in 1988. They were commenting about the value of high school for students who were academically unsuccessful or who were not going on to college:

Elsie: . . . it's a trap . . .

Alma: I think it grossly neglects them . . . [I have] . . . friends who I consider really bright . . . [high school] just didn't work for them. They had to graduate early or not graduate to get out of there. It needs . . . better counselors who don't go, if someone is feeling suicidal, go ratting on . . . telling the parents . . . I mean this is a really touchy thing, but I have friends who felt very betrayed by that and they never explained how they felt ever again. I think we need, something that Jerome was touching on, we need a system that makes you feel competent and helps you to believe in yourself . . . because if you had different standards of success . . . maybe all the teachers need to go through classes about understanding [that] human value isn't the grade point average and things like that . . . what I'm saying is that somehow we need to get away from that negative attitude . . . .I know that they are having problems with weapons and drugs in schools . . . but we don't need people patrolling the halls, acting like the students are criminals, you know, things like that, that make it such a negative environment . . . [so] that people who are on the borderline get out as soon as they can.

Jerome: School works for people . . . who are saying, okay I'm going to be part of this career oriented, goal oriented . . . society . . . [But] for kids who don't necessarily have that sort of value system . . . it doesn't. [These] kids aren't dumb. There is nothing wrong with being a carpenter and having your own pace of workmanship . . . Those values are inculcated early, I think, but school is saying that is bad in a lot of times . . .

Elsie: . . . it makes it some sort of stigma . . .

Jerome: . . . when you're different . . .

Notes

1. This sorting out/ranking process goes on throughout a student's school years. But the process is intensified at the high school level.

2. Of course there should be a great increase altogether in the number of available *academic* college scholarships based economic need. But that does not obviate my point about the importance of stressing the academic development of black kids so they can compete successfully with other kids for what academic scholarships do now exist.

3. Indeed, part of the reason there were as many black kids in the course both years as there were, was because my teaching partner and I made an effort to get the guidance counselors to find black and other minority students for the class.

9

I Have My Pass

It's the beginning of third period.

Albert, who has been absent from class for a couple of days, enters the classroom. The teacher says, in a friendly tone, "Hey Al, how are you? Where have you been?"

Al responds by saying, "I have my pass."

In fact, Al's response does not answer the question. He assumes, correctly in most cases, that the teacher does not want an answer but does want the pass. There is no communication and a good opportunity for dialogue between teacher and student is missed.

Checking and signing passes at the start of the period for kids who were absent the previous day delays getting to the job of teaching, whether that means talking with a few students about something or addressing the class as a whole. Having to check the passes of kids who are tardy disrupts the class. Both episodes are a waste of time, and make it much harder to maintain an inviting, non-confrontational classroom environment.

The system does not trust kids

Requiring passes from students reflects the fact that the system does not trust kids. It also shows the tendency of schools to set up a super-structure of non-organic rules that weigh people down. They are walls to hide behind and often serve as vehicles for Authower. Regardless of state laws on attendance, regardless of the legal fact that, in general, schools act "in loco parentis,"[1] passes not only are unnecessary for running a coherent, responsible high school, they get in the way.

More than that, they are actively harmful, further perpetuating the game of school. They impede honest relationships, honest interactions, with the students. They are not avenues, they are barriers. They block good opportunities for students and teachers to connect with each other, to talk with each other, on a human-to-human basis and not on the usual authority-to-subordinate basis.

The system conditions students and teachers not to meaningfully interact with each other, and it obligingly provides many walls for each to hide behind, of which the pass is but one. Students may be as willing as teachers not to have to deal with the reasons for their being late or absent because that often means having to talk with an adult they do not trust.

Exercising authority with passes

As with many school practices, the pass requirement is accepted by most teachers without much thought. They enforce it to various degrees. Some don't make too much of it. But for many other teachers it is of major importance. It is another way for teachers to exercise authority. They take it as a personal affront when a student is absent from their class or tardy. The pass serves as a kind of offering to The Great God Teacher—to Authower. The message to the kids, in effect, is that they do not have to deal with reasons why they were late or absent. They simply must placate the teacher with a pass.

The irony is that if a student cuts or is frequently tardy to a particular class, the reason may actually *be* a personal affront to the teacher: the kid simply can't stand going to the class. But if the teacher fixates on the pass and never tries to engage the student in a non-confrontational way about the cutting or tardiness, that teacher will never know what is bothering the student. Without some engaging of the student by the teacher, the student will likely continue to cut or be tardy, the teacher will continue demanding passes, and the game of school will go on unabated.

But the game should stop, so teachers can develop a nurturing, supportive, intellectually challenging classroom—an environment based on mutual trust, not on mutual suspicion. Passes undermine this because they are based on the assumption that students will not tell the truth about why they are absent or tardy. The assumption is that they will "take advantage" and be absent a great deal. But that was not my experience. Most of the time, if I was honest with kids, they were honest with me. Yes, sometimes it took time to create the necessary rapport, the trust, but when it happened we were free of the game.

One should not be naive. There are students who are goof-offs, who lie, who "take advantage" of the ideal classroom environment. But when one takes the risk of creating a nurturing, inviting classroom based on mutual trust, before long most of the kids who have been used to lying and goofing off will quit doing so, or do so much less. They will have less need to. This kind of an approach is more pleasant and easier than constantly having to hound kids about such foolish things as passes.

However, it is not enough simply to stop asking students for passes. Teachers must substitute for passes the active practice of engaging the students about why they were absent or tardy. Talking with students about being tardy or absent for no good reason is yet one more opportunity to build trust. Many teachers find going through the pass routine easier. Partly, this is because it becomes habitual—they don't have to think about it. Partly, it is because they don't do thinking about the rules, even rules which border on crazy.

But a major reason why many teachers find the pass routine preferable is that they are afraid to engage students. They *like* the wall the passes provide. They are afraid of losing control. Yet the opposite is true: generally, kids will respect teachers more if they feel they are being dealt with as human beings. If teachers were trained to interact with kids, and if the system encouraged this, then fears about actively engaging the kids would be much less.

Virtually any teacher would be concerned about a student who was seriously ill or in an accident. But most teachers simply don't take time to enquire about run-of-the mill absences. Moreover, in the we/they, confrontational environment of schools the tendency is to be suspicious of kids' absences. Most teachers simply do not believe students who tell them they were absent because they were sick or for some other reason considered legitimate by the system, unless the student has a pass. For most teachers the central issue is (a) that the class was missed and (b) that the school rule says the kids are supposed to have passes to enter class when tardy or absent the previous day.

Does it matter why a student is absent?

If the main concern is that by being absent from or tardy to a class a student is missing important work, then what difference does it make *why* a student is absent or tardy? That student is still absent or tardy. If, in fact, anything valuable went on in class then the student missed it regardless of the reason. So why the big deal over whether absences or tardies are for reasons the system deems as acceptable or unacceptable? The key thing is that if something went on in class that absent students should know, the teacher's job is to help those students find ways of learning what they missed. If teachers focus on the issue of absences or tardies as such, not only do they undermine an inviting classroom environment, but they waste energy and deflect themselves and their students from the main task at hand of learning and growing.

Find out for yourself

Why not use passes and engage the kids as well? Basically, if a teacher engages the kids about reasons for absences and tardies, and if the teacher maintains a nurturing environment, passes are a waste of time and paper. Besides, an element of suspicion remains.

If a teacher truly does not believe a student's reasons for being absent or tardy, she or he can investigate. The school secretary, who collects excuse notes that school rules or state law require kids to bring from home when they return after an absence, is a source of information. The person whom a student says caused the tardiness is another source. Whatever the circumstances, if it is important the teacher can take the time to get the full story of an absence or tardiness. However, the need to do this kind of checking up is rare if one has developed trust with the kids. If a teacher creates an open and mutually trusting environment, most of the behavior problems that drive teachers to distraction—such as absences and tardies—simply do not emerge, or if they do they can be handled more easily, effectively and pleasantly than with the pass routine.

There is one time when students like passes. This is when passes can be used to get them out of a class they do not want to be in. For example, if a guidance counselor sends for a student during a class, the kid can "legally" leave. This is how Leah described the feelings of many students during a boring class when someone comes into the room with a pass:

> . . . and then you're starting to look out the door . . . and someone will come into the classroom with a pass, and you're sitting there going, "Yes, it's for me. Oh, please, let it be for me." [from a 1990 audio-taped conversation with South Lakes students]

Of course, if it is an *administrator* sending for a student, in many cases the student would rather stay in class, since the usual reason for an administrator sending for a student is that the student is in some kind of trouble.

Still, these kinds of games happen very little in an inviting, non-confrontational, nurturing classroom. That kind of environment makes games unnecessary. Students do not have to waste energy finding ways to cut class or be habitually late. When they have a problem that involves not being in class, most students feel comfortable coming to the teacher to discuss the matter. The need to play games over being in class or late to class diminishes in direct proportion to the degree to which the teacher maintains a genuine learning and growing environment.

Notes

1. "In place of the parent." In most states, schools have certain powers to control students in the same way parents do. See, E. Edmund Reutter and Robert Hamilton: *The Law of Public Education*; The Foundation Press, 1970, page 514.

10

Why Didn't I Get a Better Grade?

W hy didn't I get a better grade? Was there ever a student who didn't ask this question? Or the followup, "I worked hard on that paper" or, "I studied hard for that test, I deserve a better grade." Ah, yes.

I have never met a serious, competent teacher who did not hate having to give grades. And yet giving grades is a *major* part of teaching in an American public high school. Such an integral part of one's professional life should not be something one strongly dislikes. It is not that teachers should learn to love grading. It is that grading should go.

At least it should go as it now is. We are so used to the idea of letters or numbers as symbols for telling students how well they did on a test or how good or bad is an essay they wrote, that it is hard to imagine schools without grades. Quite often students themselves are described by letter grades. Teachers will refer to Herman as an A student or Gwendolyn as a B student. It is a code most of us in this culture understand. But in fact it is not an accurate way either of evaluating student work or of describing students.

Frequent and ongoing evaluations

However, there is much pressure on teachers to grade or give marks frequently. The grading policy of the Fairfax County Public Schools is typical: "The teacher conducts frequent and ongoing evaluations in determining a quarter grade. The teacher is required to use one mark per week in determining a grade but is encouraged to use at least two marks per week."[1] Policies like this only increase the likelihood that one more inning

117

in the game of school will be played: the object becomes to give grades, not to evaluate seriously.

Saul, a 1989 South Lakes graduate, wrote an interesting comment in his alumni survey response on how concern over grades can cause students to play the game:

> The least valuable academic experience in H.S was how one perceives the emphasis of grades. When planning one's schedule, it is difficult not to weigh two similar courses (one GT, one not) and ponder one's grade. As the senior year approaches and colleges begin calling, I'm sure many students are infected with a type of "grade-itis" in which they take an easier course to pull an "A" and boost their GPA [grade point average] . . . The structure of education discourages challenging oneself, for the *end results* (the grade) [Saul's emphasis] are how a student is judged.

Saul also had a good comment on the relationship between the frequency of testing, and learning:

> . . . I found that in the classes in which tests were given very frequently, my focus was not on the information/learning but only on attaining the good grades. Conversely, in those classes in which only a few tests were given (although these tests were worth more), the greater time between tests/quizzes allowed the subject matter to be appreciated for its own sake . . . my worst learning situations in H.S were those classes that tested too frequently, [that] emphasized testing. This caused only the test grade received to be emphasized and not the learning.

Why is giving grades so distasteful?

There are three reasons.

● The first is that to reduce the value of student work to a letter or a number demeans the work. All the effort and thought that went into the essay or research paper, all that was learned while working on it, and the value of the final product, are being summed up in a single letter or number. One single letter or number cannot possibly reflect all that. Even a single letter or number grade for a quiz or test does not reflect the thought that may have gone into studying for the quiz or test.

Moreover, the letter or number grade does not reflect what the student knows; only what the student does not know. Tony may have gotten 25% of the answers on a test wrong, and so his percentage grade is 75%, a letter grade of C, an "average" grade. But in fact, *he got 75% of the answers correct*. Yet this is not reflected in the number/letter grade. Why is knowing three-fourths of the answers considered "average?" It is only "average" if the basis for evaluation is that the biggest bulk of the students get 75%. If, instead, the basis for evaluation is the number of correct answers against the total number of possible correct answers, a score of 75% might be very good, or not very good, depending on the nature of the test.

The bell-shaped curve

Put another way, the decision to give a score of 75% a letter grade of C (average) is made before the test is given. It has nothing to do with evaluating students in terms of how many correct answers they got out of the total of correct answers possible. It is based on the assumption that the bulk of the students will get a score in the 75% range. This, in turn, is based on an invalid adaptation of the normal or bell-shaped curve used in statistics for measuring large blocks of a whole population. The assumption of the normal curve is that in a very large population a few will do extremely well at some task, a few extremely poorly and the rest will be scattered in between along the curve with the biggest group near the top of the bell.

In applying this concept to a class of students the assumption is that all the students taking a test will fall into the five traditional grade categories of A,B,C,D,F which are plotted along the curve. The biggest bulk of kids (about 40%) will be in the middle. These are the students who get the "average" grade of around 75%—a C. The rest fall into each of the other grade categories, with about 10% each in the A and F categories—at each end of the curve—and about 20% each in the B & D categories—on either side of the C category on the curve.

It is not reasonable to adapt the curve idea to a class-sized population of students. There are too many variables left out. One is that the particular mix of students may or may not be an accurate sampling of the total population. Nor does using this curve approach to grading students take into account the fairness of the exam, the environment of the class, the students' relationship to the teacher, how well prepared the students are, the weight given to the exam in the final grade for a course, and so forth.

In effect, what happens in the typical way tests (or anything else) are graded, is that, regardless of any of these other variables, 75% is "average," 85% is "above average" (B), and 95% is "excellent" (A). So, before the test is even taken by the students the grading decision is made that only 20–30% of the students are "above average" or better. Why is this necessarily so? There is no inherent reason for such an assumption other than a dim view of the potential of most students, most people.

119

What does this say about the relationship between how well a teacher teaches and how well students learn? Doesn't the fact that most students get 75% or better on an exam say that most learned quite well and that, probably, the teacher taught well? Why is 75% not very good at least? Of course, it is hard to make this judgement without knowing variables such as those noted above. And that is part of the point: grading scales should not be based primarily on the number of students who get a particular grade—a crude, invalid adaptation of the so-called bell curve. That is not reasonable. Grades, if they must exist, should be based on how many correct answers students got out of the total number possible. And then deciding how many of those answers constitute a so-called "average" or "above average" or "excellent" grade should be made after taking into account the variables such as those noted above. There is no inherent reason why 75% should be an average grade.

Who's good at what?

One might argue that a sorting out/ranking function is necessary in society to determine who is good or not good at various skills and occupations. That is true. It is important to have ways of discovering who is good at various skills and occupations. But grading as we now do it does not fill this need. Much more effective are evaluation via apprenticeship programs and other tools that truly focus on what people have learned and are good at.[2] The evaluation process should be a serious collaborative effort between teacher and student in which the aim is to help people learn and grow in as many areas as they can and want to. It should not focus exclusively on tests graded on what percent of those taking them get a certain score—and tests which primarily test the ability to take a test.

● The second reason grading is distasteful is that it causes, or at least strongly encourages, students to work primarily for the grade. Watch what happens when a teacher returns to students a set of essays or a test. The first things the kids do are (a) look for the grade they received and (b) ask each other what grade they got. Then, depending on the class and the teacher, the students might read the comments the teacher made on the paper.

Kids aren't fooled

Students are not fooled by grades. They tolerate them because they feel they have no choice; they are conditioned to do so. This is especially true for college-bound students who feel keenly the need to have good grades to qualify. But they understand that it undermines learning. As

Kate Sproul, a 1989 South Lakes graduate, said on her alumni survey response:

> Students that are going on to college have to get good grades. Students who show their parents their report cards have to get good grades. We learn when we first start school to focus on grades and forget about how much we learn.

Students who, early in their school lives, have been labeled C, D or F students simply give up on grades, more or less accepting their fates. They usually don't even try to play the game to get good grades, figuring it won't work anyway, so why bother. As one student said on a 1990 Government course evaluation:

> Grades simply promote competition and turn off many students.

● The third reason giving grades is distasteful is that it is destructive. It is one more barrier in the student-teacher relationship. Unless the teacher works to overcome the barrier, there always is lurking in the mind of the student, "you have my fate in your hands." It is difficult to develop an honest, mutually satisfying relationship with a student under these circumstances. Perhaps this is inevitable, given the subordinate/authoritative nature of a student-teacher relationship. It could be argued that such a subordinate/authority relationship in teaching kids is a good idea; that it preserves the distance necessary between teacher and student. But I do not think so.

Whatever distance between teacher and student may be necessary should not be built on a foundation of fear or threat. Given the incredible weight put on grades by the system, and hence by most kids and their parents, the teacher's grading power easily becomes something for the kids to fear. Teachers do not need the power of grades to maintain their status. In fact, it gets in the way of their becoming the kinds of teachers they should be: people with more experience, maturity and probably knowledge than the students, whose job is to help them find ways to learn and grow.

What authority and distance a teacher may need to help kids learn should come from a relationship of mutual respect. It is obvious to the kids that the teacher is older and has more information. For many teachers, giving grades is less an evaluation tool than it is an exercise of power— part of Authower. No doubt many teachers will say that this is an unfair and untrue statement. But the evidence from student comments over many years supports it. This relates to why so many kids feel alienated from academic learning.

Should student work be evaluated? Of course it should and must be evaluated. If a student says that 2 and 2 is 3, or spells "too" when it should be "two," or says that New York is the capital of the United States, the teacher should not ignore it, or praise the student for trying without also finding an effective way of helping the student see the error. Essays and other longer work also deserve an honest critique. It is vital that a teacher seriously evaluate the work. The issue is not whether to evaluate but how: what are the criteria and the context for the evaluation? What is the real purpose?

The real purpose of evaluation

Do we evaluate truly to help the student learn and grow? Or do we evaluate to exercise Authower? Or do we evaluate with a letter or number grade because it is easier and the system tells us we must? The system feeds the expectations of most students and parents who assume that learning can and should be evaluated with a letter or a number. But there are better ways.

For example, when a student writes a two- or three-page essay or an eight- to 12-page research paper, the teacher reads it carefully, making comments and corrections throughout. The teacher evaluates the paper by noting any incorrect spelling or grammar, by asking where the citation for a quote is, by noting the ways in which a particular paragraph makes great sense, or noting a paragraph that makes no sense. Then, at the end of the paper, the teacher sums up his or her general reactions to it and makes general suggestions to help the student improve writing and analysis in the future. But then after seriously and thoroughly evaluating the paper, the teacher reduces all that to a B+, or whatever. Why? Why? It is crazy. There simply is no rational reason for the letter/number grade. Why not just consider the evaluation to be the many corrections and comments throughout the paper?

The system's answer is that the students must be given number/letter grades on papers, tests, and so forth, so that they may be averaged to create a final grade for the course. But who says we need to give grades for the course? At most we should be making all courses pass/fail. But to do that would alter radically the school's self-appointed sorting out/ranking function.

Teaching—and learning—to a letter or number grade is the pedagogical equivalent of the sound bite political advertising held in such poor repute for its over use on television. Superficially, teaching/learning to a grade does work, as does the sound-bite, superficially. It may force some students to study and work. But it does not help them to actually learn. It does not help them to develop a life-long desire to learn and grow, to truly evaluate the ideas of others, to be able to stand for something and not just be victims of, well, of sound bites.

A radical step

It is radical to eliminate letter/number grades and substitute written evaluations. Within the present structure of public high schools it would require several changes in attitude and behavior. Teachers would have to be trained and willing to evaluate seriously via comments and forgo just putting numbers or letters on student work. The system would have to support it. It would mean convincing students and parents that this makes sense. It would mean kids would have to comprehend the teacher's evaluation; they could no longer play the game of "I got a B, what did you get?" with other kids.

Abandoning letter or number grading would cause significant changes in the mechanisms for evaluating student work. Paper-and-pencil tests would be used as educational tools, not primarily as tools for judgement. That is, the purpose of the tests and quizzes would be to see what the kids know as the course progresses. They would help pinpoint what else they need to know to complete the course as successfully as possible. There would be more essays. And there would be more oral examination of students in which teachers could discuss with students any errors made in solving a math problem or conducting a science experiment, or writing an essay, and help them at the moment.

This approach also would mean fewer formal evaluations—less frequent tests and quizzes that receive letter/number grades. It makes no sense to give students grades once or twice a week, let alone daily, as many teachers do and as the system encourages or requires. It further undermines genuine learning and growth.

Kids need feedback

However, giving grades should not be confused with giving informal feedback to kids, and commenting to them on how they are doing in the course. Teachers should frequently give this feedback to kids and encourage them to seek it. Giving feedback in informal ways and in a non-confrontational, nurturing environment does not present the same threat as constant, frequent grades. It provides another way for teachers and students to interact around what should be the central purpose of school: learning and growing.[3]

Finally, this proposed change would also require that colleges and employers be willing to accept transcripts of students with teacher comments as the evaluation rather than the present system of transcripts of grades.

Perhaps a start toward eliminating grades has been made in allowing students to take some elective courses on a pass/fail basis, now quite common in high schools. Some of the grading pressure is off in a pass/fail course, since at least in theory a student would only have to get what might conventionally be considered a D to pass. But even pass/fail courses do not completely remove the grade threat. Nor do such courses insure that useful evaluation and feedback will be given to students by the teacher. Here, too, the teachers must be trained and supported in different ways of evaluating the students' work.

Moreover, if this idea were extended to all courses, it would require most of the changes in behavior and attitude noted above. But having students take all courses on a pass/fail basis, would make a start in discovering that more genuine learning occurs without the use of the judgmental tool of letter/number grades.

Obviously, trying to do all this will not be an easy task, given the present structure and values of the system. At the very least, we must take seriously the damage that grades do to genuine learning. We must work toward developing an evaluation system that truly evaluates what students know, and what they need and want to know. We need an evaluation system that encourages kids to learn and grow.

Notes

1. FCPS Regulation 2430.1P, 1987
2. Evaluation techniques are discussed more in Chapters 11 and 13.
3. This approach to grading also would be much easier if the teacher-student ratio were better, so that teachers could concentrate more on fewer students. The relationship between student-teacher ratio and alternative ways of testing are discussed in later chapters.

11

The Testing Game

Do tests demonstrate that students actually know and understand the material for which they are tested? Probably not. So why are they the main way students are evaluated?

Here is an interesting response to that question from two South Lakes seniors who participated in a 1990 audio-taped discussion:

Joe: As near as I can tell, tests aren't for the teachers to find out what the student knows; tests are used to threaten kids. Like, when we have a quiz in Chemistry, it's "Quiz on Friday, on chapters 1 and 2." So you have to read chapters 1 and 2 by Friday . . .

Leah: Right. There's something that Joe's getting at . . . that when [a teacher] says that to you, you read it the night before . . . and you forget it as soon as you take the test. And that's not learning, that's cramming information in . . .

What are tests?

"Tests" are the standard tools which are supposed to determine if students know material they have been assigned to learn: multiple-choice tests, true-and-false tests, short-answer tests, essay tests. Though there are wide variations among these standard measurement tools, there are important commonalities among them, too.

All of these tests assume the teacher and teacher-assigned textbook have all the answers and that the object for students is to show that they learned these answers. With few exceptions high school students are required to take the tests in a set time frame such as a class period or less. Tests are almost always taken individually—students are not to talk with each other or exchange written information while taking the test. And, tests are usually graded along lines discussed in the previous chapter.

Joe and Leah, quoted above, attested to their perceptions that tests are mostly a spitting back of memorized material, often soon forgotten. Here is an especially incisive comment about the value of tests compared to writing papers as an evaluation instrument. Trent, a 1989 South Lakes graduate, said this in a 1991 audio-taped conversation:

> Instead of tests, instead of Scantron tests [machine-scored tests], writing papers [is better], because papers require thinking and tests require memorization. So if you're doing a paper you have to pull together information and come up with a conclusion, whereas if you're taking a test, you just have to repeat other peoples' conclusions. And when people go on to business or college, or wherever they go, they're not asked to repeat other peoples' conclusions, they're asked to take the information and come up with their own. If they're working for IBM, if someone asks their opinion, they're not going to be expected to say, well, you know, this is the most correct answer. You know, 95 percent of the public *believes* this [Trent's emphasis]. What they're going to be expected to deliver is an analysis of the information, and that's what papers begin to do. In high school students aren't . . . now . . . aren't used to writing, but as soon as they get to college, they're expected to write.

Trent's perception about the value of multiple-choice tests is supported by an interesting experiment run by James Herbert Shea with his earth-science classes. After the students turned in "their usual short-answer and essay exam," Shea writes,

> I gave them a multiple-choice exam to complete. The second exam had 15 to 21 of the identical questions they had just answered, only this time in multiple-choice format with four possible answers for each question. The result was . . . *the students scored 43 percent higher on the multiple-choice exam than they did on the identical questions in short-answer format* [Shea's emphasis] . . .[1]

Shea was disturbed by what these results said about the value of multiple-choice tests. On quite a few questions, students could pick out correct answers from a list but could not come up with correct answers when confronted with a question that required them to wrestle with an answer. Shea concluded:

> The end result of my little experiment was that I am more convinced than ever that multiple-choice test results are extremely misleading and that too many instructors have allowed the convenience and efficiency of multiple-choice exams to lead them down the slippery slope of . . . counterfeit education.[2]

But, while the problem is worse with multiple-choice tests than with essay or short-answer tests, there is a larger question that must be answered: what do *any* tests tell us?

You cannot test for understanding

They *may* accurately reflect what a student knows about a particular subject *at the moment the test is taken*. But by their very nature tests cannot reflect whether or not the student truly understands the material, let alone knows how to make use of it—as Trent said. They do not give either the student or the teacher useful information.

The value of tests has been analyzed and discussed by many educators and scholars developing alternative ways for learning whether students understand material they have been studying. I add my voice to those educators and scholars who question or totally oppose the use of tests as the primary evaluation tool.

If tests are of such limited value, why do they remain the primary means of evaluation in most high schools? There are several reasons.

Tests support the system's sorting out/ranking function, discussed in chapter 8. Tests maintain the illusion that those who do well on tests are the more talented students—the future leaders, as it is often put. More likely, however, they are the ones better able to pass tests. They may or may not be students who can think effectively, are truly knowledgeable, and understand concepts—the tools through which knowledge is used and expanded. Students who pass tests may or may not be the ones who question, who are creative, who are self-directed, who are able and willing to be active, coherent participants in this democracy.

Tests and parents

Tests also support the essentially conservative and frequently self-serving nature of public high schools. Their results can easily be used to measure the worth of the school and give the appearance that the school is doing its job.

Parents are used to tests and generally feel comfortable with them. What parents may not see is the way teachers and administrators hide behind test results as a way of keeping angry or upset parents at bay: "Your son is a behavior problem," Mrs. Akynoma, "he does not do his work—why, just look at his test scores." The test scores thus become a kind of shield between parent and educator—after all, how can a parent argue with test scores? This function of scores is similar to that of passes between student and teacher. In each case, the written item substitutes for honest interaction. In the case of test scores, an opportunity is lost for creating a we/we environment in which student, teacher and parent co-operate to find out why, for example, Mrs. Akynoma's son is a so-called behavior problem.

Certainly teachers generally are comfortable with tests. In addition to being able to use test results as shields against angry parents, most tests are easier to correct and assign letter or number grades than are more complicated evaluation tools such as essays.

Though they may dislike taking tests and often correctly see them as merely the spitting back of memorized material, most students also are comfortable with tests. They are accustomed to them. Indeed, students often initially resist alternative ways of evaluating what they have learned, fearing these ways—at least until they get used to them.

The game of tests

Unequivocally, test-taking in schools is a game. It is a destructive, unnecessary game. What makes tests a game is the context in which they are given, the way they are graded, the weight put on them and the perception of their results. Testing is a game because its real purposes are not made clear. And, ironically, testing in fact does not show what kids truly understand and whether they know how to use and build upon the tested material.

But why should we be surprised at all this? After all, if school in general is a game, why would testing be different? The nature of the system insures that tests are part of the game. If schools do not encourage students to be involved in the process of their own learning, it follows that students are also not involved in the evaluation of their work. Tests are simply another way of keeping students passive: Kim studies for a test and passes it. Whether or not she understands does not matter. Neither the test nor the system asks her to understand. What matters is that she got a test result. Unless it is not as good as she thinks it should be, that will keep Kim quiet, and she will go on to the next event until she finally graduates, or leaves.

In fact, in no part of the educational process does the game become more evident than in testing. In no part of the process does the we/they environment exist more strongly. As tests are usually constructed and given in high schools, they are per force a contest between teacher and students. "This is what I told you to learn," says the teacher. "And this test shows I learned it," says the student. "Maybe," says the teacher, who has the final word.

Making test-taking an individual matter (no talking during the test), and pressuring students to do well, virtually guarantees that cheating will go on. Many kids see the test as a challenge, not just to their ability to spit back information but to their ability to cheat effectively. Students learn to be test-wise, as they learn to be teacher-wise. Most of those who consistently do well on tests are those who have learned how to take tests. They may or may not also actually know the material or understand its use. But they also know that understanding does not matter—that is not why they are being tested. The game continues among the students when the test results are announced —from comparing test results with each other to complaining that they did not get the grades they should have.

Most kids understand this as a game but feel obligated to play it: their futures, college admissions, and more are at risk if they do not—and they are right, given the way the system works.

But where kids can revolt, they do. One place is in the various standardized achievement tests given system-wide to students at certain grade levels. Schools try to get students to take these kinds of tests seriously, for their results are used as a measure of the schools' performance and of how well the teachers are teaching. The results of these kinds of tests are also often used by real estate agents to convince prospective house buyers with kids how good the school district is. But the kids see it differently when they realize that these tests have little to do with them and nothing to do with whether or not they get into a college or get a job. Then students—especially the older ones—don't take the tests seriously. Many make little effort to be careful with their answers. I saw this many times as a teacher. My perception is supported by this item from New York *Times* Education section:[3]

> *Torrance, Calif., May 2 (AP):* Seniors at a top-performing high school in this Los Angeles suburb sabotaged their answers on a recent annual test that measures schools' academic quality.
>
> One of the students says the diminished scores were a rebellion against pressure to perform. But administrators at the school, West High, deny there was too much pressure . . .
>
> West High School's reading scores in the test dropped from the 85th percentile statewide last year to the 51st this year, and mathematics scores fell from the 95th percentile to the 71st percentile.
>
> William Bawden, the school's principal, said a check of

students' test booklets, which are not signed, had shown an unusual number of wrong answers in 18 booklets, including some booklets that contained no right answers. He said one student had admitted deliberately doing poorly.

The student body president, Kelly Price, said some seniors became disgruntled when teachers interrupted classes to prepare students for the test and when administrators visited classes to stress the importance of doing well on it.

Involving students

It is as important to involve students in the process of their own assessment—evaluation—as it is in the process of their own learning. Serious assessment is an integral part of learning. But students rarely see it that way, since they see the usual assessment tool—the test—as a club and a game.

Students should be involved with the evaluation process of determining if they do understand material they have studied. That process should not be a contest between student and teacher. It should not be used to give the appearance that some students have learned something and others have not, or to sort and rank students. The assessment should be a collaborative effort between students and teachers, and, where it is appropriate, parents also should be involved. To do this, of course, means abandoning or radically curtailing the current system of giving grades. There is no reason to assume that achievement will always be distributed on a bell curve, where X percent of students must get high grades, Y percent must get poor grades and Z percent must fail.

In their book, *Portfolio Assessment in the Reading-Writing Classroom*,[4] Robert J. Tierney, Mark A. Carter and Laura E. Desai discuss at length the problems with conventional testing. And while they are concerned in the book with assessing students' learning how to read and write, what they say is applicable to any discipline. While not specifically calling testing a game, the problems with testing these authors identify point to a game.

Tierney, et al, very much assume that assessment must involve students and teachers collaboratively:

> . . . assessment [should have] a working relationship with teaching and learning. We believe that assessment should empower teachers, students and parents; that worthwhile classroom practices should be ignited and not extinguished by assessment; and that students should view assessment as an opportunity to reflect upon and

celebrate their effort, progress, and improvement, as well as their processes and products.[5]

Hurray! What a fine statement of what assessment should be.

There is no quick, easy way of changing assessment practices within the system as it is. But there are various kinds of things teachers can do to mitigate the damage from testing.

Tests must be fair

On the simplest level, teachers can make sure tests, as well as grades, are fair. With tests this means trying to make sure that the questions are not petty. Do not ask students about unimportant details to try to trick them, a not uncommon practice. With grades this usually means giving students the higher grade if their numerical averages were on the border between two grades. But of course such efforts are likely to be inconsistent, will not always work, and will not address the basic problem of tests or of letter/number grades.

Another thing teachers can do is give equal weight to a whole variety of assessment tools in addition to conventional tests: essays (both those written in class as part of a test and those done at home), class discussions which reveal what students know, oral presentations, individual conferences in which students are quizzed about some topic. While time-consuming, the individual conference is an especially valuable tool.[6] Once students get over being afraid to talk privately for five or ten minutes with the teacher in an interchange that allows students to elaborate on answers, they usually like this approach to assessment. Helping students overcome fears about private conferences is part of creating a nurturing, non-confrontational, we/we environment.

Untimed tests

Something that can be done to reduce the unnecessary pressure of taking tests is to make them untimed. This means that the kids know at the start of a test designed to take the whole period that if they need more time to finish they can have it. This can be done either by allowing students to stay after the period is over, if their schedule permits, or coming back after school to finish the test. Not too many students took advantage of this option when I offered it, but some did. However, many students told me that knowing they had as much time as they needed helped relax them so they could actually be more efficient in taking the test than they otherwise might be.

Why must tests be done within a certain time frame? One big reason is teacher/administrative convenience. While this is an understandable concern for teachers, it should not be the determining factor in the process of effectively evaluating what students know. Another big reason is the fear that students will cheat if teachers let them return later to complete a test. Given the establishment of the kind of teacher-student relationship I know is possible, this is rarely an issue. Students do not take the test with them, anyway.

So, what does it prove that Cynthia or Evan can take a test faster than can Dionne or Max? Does a timed test tell us anything more about what the student knows? Not so far as I can tell.

Another assessment device is an oral exam of the whole class at once. In this situation the teacher asks questions about material the students were to have covered for that day, selecting at random students to answer. If a given student doesn't know the answer, the teacher goes to another student and returns later to the first student for another question. This approach has its risks, of course. Students who are unprepared are put on the spot and students who do not get a chance to answer but who knew the answer are disappointed. But, again, in a nurturing environment these kinds of risks are minimal—especially if the kids also know that the teacher is not putting too much weight on the results of this kind of assessment, but rather is using it as one of many tools of assessment.[7]

Raising the raw score

A long-standing technique used by teachers to off-set bad test results is to raise the raw scores students receive on a test by either some percentage number or by an absolute number of points—say, everyone gets a 10 percent increase in points, or 5 additional points, resulting in a higher number of kids getting better grades than would otherwise be the case. Some teachers do this especially if the test results for a particular class are not what the teacher thinks they should be. However, while the kids do not object when a teacher raises test result numbers, doing so does not change the basic problem of testing—or grading.

Nor do adding points or assigning higher grades to test results deal with such other matters as how the test is written and what its true function is. Are the test questions written in such a way as to virtually ensure that only a handful of students will be able to answer them? That test is designed to perpetuate the system's ranking function. If one assumes that it is "natural" for only 10 percent of the students to get an A, and only 20 percent to get a B, and so forth, then the test will be written to get that result.

Self-evaluation

One other assessment tool that can be used within the constraints of the current system is to have the students perform a self-evaluation. For example, near the end of each marking period, students can be asked to respond to two or three general questions designed to get them to examine their own involvement and performance in the course for that grading period. Then, students can be asked to assign themselves number grades [85%, 90%, etc.], which might count for some percentage of their total grade for that marking period. In my classes the students' self-evaluation grade counted for 25% of their total grade. The students must also explain on their self-evaluations why they gave themselves that grade. Their grades can be averaged into the teacher's grades, thus allowing the students to be involved in the decision about their grades. This also is a way of giving students experience in self-direction, and helping them become self-aware.

Students have to be convinced about the value of self-evaluation. The teacher must accept that it will take time for the process to work well, and for students to learn to take it seriously. Discussions with them about the whole concept of self-evaluation is part of creating a we/we environment. And in that environment there is every reason for the students to be honest.

When first told about this kind of self-evaluation, many students say that everyone will give themselves an A. There is a three-fold answer the teacher can give the students. One, is that kids are honest if the teacher is honest with them. Actually, students often undervalue themselves. Also, one can ask the kids, so what if students give themselves an A? If that is how they feel about their involvement in the course, then that is what they should put down. It is, after all, *their* self-assessment. Finally, one can remind the students that while they have 25% of the grade, the teacher has 75%—so in this model of grading, power is still weighted in favor of the teacher!

Kids *are* honest. By the second quarterly marking period, students can make good use of this self-growth tool. Most see that the purpose of the self-evaluation is not only for grading. It is yet another way for them to learn and grow. It is another way for teachers and students to interact. When I used this system, I did not just record the grades students gave themselves. I always read what students wrote and responded to it before returning the self-evaluations.

Here is a sampling of four students' self-evaluations from the third quarter of the 1985–86 school year:

> At this point in government class, I feel less afraid to participate in class discussions. I am a lot more informed with world wide problems and definitely more interested and concerned. I *want* to participate rather than know I *have* to be graded on a certain test which I'll probably forget the next day. [Justine; the emphases are hers.]

> For the first time in my life I realize that I am not giving at all enough attention to my school work . . . this quarter I have not given 100% on any government project, or any other school project for that matter. I pay attention . . . only when I feel like it, which is a very poor attitude. It is for these reasons that I feel I deserve a 70%, or D, for the quarter. [Perry, a very bright, very turned-off young man who began to reassess himself as his comments indicate.]

> This quarter I functioned well, but it was not as good as second quarter. I asked questions when something was unclear to me and . . . made comments when I felt I had something to add to the class. [But] I did complete [all my work] as carefully . . . as I have previously. I slacked off this quarter. [Neal]

> I think a little differently about people [in the class], their opinions and what I feel about those opinions. Instead of following my first impression and labeling a comment as "_____," I think about the comment and why the person may have said it, instead of judging the person in the beginning . . . [so] I think (Yes! Actually think!) about my reactions and comments more than I used to. [Maggie]

But helpful as these various possibilities are to mitigate the damage of testing, they are all gimmicks—arms and legs stuck on the body of the school system as it is. Even the self-evaluation, which comes closest to being the kind of evaluation/assessment experience that ought to be the norm, is a gimmick. It is still tied to a number/letter grade and the grading power still rests with the teacher. But at least it allows the student some opportunity to buy into the grading system on his or her own terms. Still, the game goes on, the system's sorting out/ranking function is still in place. More basic and radical evaluation proposals that eliminate the game are discussed in chapter 13.

In response to the question, "What are the most valuable academic experiences you had in high school?" this student said on a 1990 South Lakes student survey:

> . . . realizing that school is all about grades and no substance is really involved. Improvising and grabbing things out of the air is a main way of doing work and doing it that way is the most bearable way of doing it.

In April 1990 several of my government students attended a conference in Washington, D.C., designed for high school students. Mike Kochenash's reaction to the experience is a fine commentary on learning, and on serious evaluation vs. conventional testing:

> . . . the *Budget Puzzle Conference* . . . was a wonderful opportunity . . . At first I had my doubts about how I would fare . . . I was intimidated by the knowledge that the conference would contain some of the brightest students from around the country. I didn't think I had learned enough in government this year to be able to participate on a comparable level with these students. Sure we discussed many relevant topics in class and I had written papers dealing with the budget and trade deficits but we did not follow the typical method of learning. We didn't read a chapter from the textbook, discuss it in class Monday, answer 45 review questions about it for homework, turn the questions in for a grade on Tuesday, go over them on Wednesday, have a test on Thursday, and then repeat the entire process with subsequent chapters week after week . . . I was pleasantly surprised when I discovered that not only could I actively participate in my group's discussion, but that I was leading that discussion . . . I am not saying that I was smarter than the other students, but that I had *learned* more about the budget problems and possible solutions than they had . . . Through attending the conference I realized that I actually learned a lot more than I thought I had in government class . . . I feel that [my participation in] the Conference was an infinitely more valuable assessment of my knowledge than any traditional exam because *I learned that I had learned* and that I could use what I had learned in advanced intellectual situations on the spur of the moment. This is much more important to me than memorizing often trivial facts that are regurgitated on test day and then mostly forgotten because they are never used afterwards . . . [emphases are Mike's]

Notes

1. This editorial originally appeared in the September 1992 issue of the *Journal of Geo-*

logical Education and was reprinted in the January 1993 issue of *The Physics Teacher*, page 8.

2. Ibid.

3. May 3, 1989, p. 21; quoted in Tierney, Carter and Desai: *Portfolio Assessment in the Reading-Writing Classroom* [Norwood, MA: Christopher-Gordon Publishers, 1991], pp. 33–34.

4. Christopher-Gordon Publishers, 1991

5. Ibid., page 21

6. I found that meeting with students periodically this way was enormously helpful in determining what they knew or did not know about something. Sometimes, I would devote all or part of several class periods to meeting with kids in this way, while the class as a whole did other work, or while some went to the library. I also scheduled individual conferences before and after school, sometimes at lunch and sometimes at my house at night when that was the only way I could meet with some kids.

7. I found this approach not always successful for an interesting reason. A given question, or response from a student, would generate a good class discussion and we never would get back to the 'exam' that day. That sometimes the kids would deliberately get me off on a discussion to stop the exam did not alter the fact that the discussions often were top-notch. I did not use this assessment approach all that often, but when I did it was useful.

12

Why Can't School Be Like TV?

Why, indeed? After all, TV is much more fun and much less demanding than school and gives the appearance of teaching the viewer information. It has become so much a part of our lives that we inhale it like the air. And, like the air, it may be far more dangerous to our well-being than we want to admit. But there is no doubt that television has had a profound and mostly negative impact on schools and students, teaching and learning. Why is this so and what can be done about it?

What's wrong with TV?

Most discussion of television revolves around the issue of its quality: good versus bad programs, too much violence or explicit sex, and so forth. And for kids, especially, there are additional questions of quantity. How much TV should kids watch? Do they watch too much? Should they watch TV at all? While quality and quantity issues are important, Neil Postman, Professor of Communication Arts & Sciences at New York University, has pinpointed a more fundamental factor: that the main issue about television is not its quality or quantity but its existence.

Postman's superb book, *Amusing Ourselves To Death*[1] is very useful for understanding the impact of television on education.[2] Of course, Postman analyzes the impact of television generally and its major role in creating, and in preparing people for, what has become America's "fun-loving culture," to use his phrase. In turn, Postman correctly recognizes that other new technology (such as the computer) also has radically altered our culture. Certainly the impact of modern technology on the society in general, as well as the impact of our technologically fueled, hedonistic value system, is the context for television's impact on education. This chapter concentrates on TV's impact on education, using Postman's analysis as a framework for my own.

Postman identifies the central problem with TV: that it is above all an entertainment medium. Whether the show is obvious entertainment or the nightly news or a serious documentary on an important public issue, TV programs must be packaged as entertainment to capture and hold an audience.[3] In fact, Postman argues that so-called serious television may be worse precisely because it is easier to be fooled that one has been informed and enlightened and not primarily entertained. "We would all be better off if television got worse, not better," he argues. "*The A-Team* and *Cheers* are no threat to our public health. *60 Minutes*, *Eye-Witness News* and *Sesame Street* are."[4]

But whether billed as serious or not, TV shows must be fast-paced and sure-footed. In fact, Postman argues that:

> When a television show is in process, it is very nearly impermissible to say "Let me think about that" or "I don't know" . . . This type of discourse not only slows down the tempo of the show but creates the impression of uncertainty . . . It tends to reveal people in the *act of thinking* [Postman's emphasis], which is as disconcerting and boring on television as it is on a Las Vegas stage.[5]

Postman looks specifically at the issue of TV and education in a chapter entitled, "Teaching As An Amusing Activity." Here, he highlights the relationship between teaching and entertainment.

> Television's principal contribution to educational philosophy is the idea that teaching and entertainment are inseparable, . . . This entirely original conception is to be found nowhere else in educational discourses . . . You will find it said by some that children will learn best when they are interested in what they are learning . . . that reason is best cultivated when it is rooted in robust emotional ground. You will even find some who say that learning is best facilitated by a loving and benign teacher. But no one has ever said or implied that significant learning is effectively, durably and truthfully achieved when education is entertainment.[6]

Let me entertain you

This speaks to a dilemma faced by serious teachers: how to combine being interesting enough to the kids to grab their attention and yet get them to be serious and take learning seriously. Needing to grab students' attention is not a result of television. Good teachers have always been good actors. But TV has markedly intensified that aspect of teaching.

As Postman says, an understanding of the importance of kids' interest in what they learn, and of the role of the teacher in the process, is not new. What *is* new is that TV has greatly intensified in kids the notion that school must *constantly* be fun and that *all* assignments should be fun. The role of teacher as entertainer has been heightened. Having fun is a critical barometer of student feeling about school. Ask most students what they think of a course and, in addition to telling you what they think of the teacher they will tell you if the course is fun or not. Kids do want to feel they have learned, but they want it to be fun. "For me," said one student on a June 1990 government course evaluation, "it [a mock trial done in class] was both fun and interesting because I was involved, which helped me to understand not just memorize." This is a wonderfully positive statement which reflects the value the student puts on learning, but notice that fun is an important ingredient. One sees the fun factor also in the responses of former students who have gone on to college. When asked how college is going, the typical response is something like, "it's fun" or "the courses are fun" or, "the courses are not fun."

Now, I am not a sourpuss who does not like fun. I think fun is wonderful and vital. And for young people to want things to be fun is natural. It certainly pre-dates TV. But the fun factor has been significantly heightened by TV's influence, largely because students, like people generally, have become used to almost constant entertainment. Students certainly are capable of learning without being entertained. But getting them to learn seriously has become much more difficult under TV's influence. In effect, kids want school to be like TV. Or, at least, they assume TV as the model for learning. This is not as far-fetched as it may sound. Television has significantly changed our assumptions about learning and has become successful competition for schools. Shows like " . . . 'Cheers' and 'The Tonight Show' . . . are as effective as 'Sesame Street' in promoting what might be called the television style of learning," says Postman. "And this style of learning is, by its nature, hostile to what has been called book-learning or its hand-maiden, school-learning."[7] Moreover, while some information may be learned from these shows, they are primarily entertainment. They are primarily fun.

So there is a dilemma even for teachers who are "loving and benign." It is fun to amuse kids. It is part of the joy in working with young people. And amusing them does grab their attention and often provides a vehicle to tap their interest in the subject at hand. Unfortunately the line between tapping students' interest in the subject at hand and making an assignment fun for its own sake is sometimes thin, as is the line between a loving and benign teacher and a teacher who is mainly an entertainer. The dilemma—the challenge—is how to move from using fun as a gimmick for getting kids' attention to having them take seriously the subject to be learned.

Packaging learning

Postman pinpoints part of the problem when he talks about the danger of packaging learning in a media format, that is, as entertainment. He discusses at length an elaborate and costly television program called "The Voyage of the Mimi." Produced in the early 1980s, it was designed to teach kids science and math in an entertaining way. Postman asks:

> . . . [I]n the end, what will the students have learned? They will, to be sure, have learned something about whales, perhaps about navigation and map reading, most of which they could have learned just as well by other means. Mainly, they will have learned that learning is a form of entertainment or, more precisely, that anything worth learning can take the form of an entertainment, and ought to.[8]

The fact is, however, that when working with a wide variety of students, 25 to 30 at a time five times a day, teachers often feel an almost desperate need to truly reach students. They want them to take learning seriously, to buy into their own learning, to overcome the feeling of so many kids that school is tedious, boring and irrelevant to them. Since students do learn more of enduring value when they become involved and interested, it seems valid to use virtually any technique that may be necessary to gain their attention. This may mean the teacher simply being funny sometimes. It also may mean using techniques that are enjoyable but are not, of themselves, the substance of the lesson. These techniques include activities such as simulation games, plays, role-playing and field trips. Even debating, though ostensibly more serious than these other projects, is often an enjoyable activity that can get students involved and learning.

These kinds of activities are not merely fun and games. They provide a bridge to learning substance that is often missing when the teacher tries to get the students into a topic with a straight no-nonsense lecture or textbook assignment. Over and over again kids have said that using these varied kinds of activities does enable them to learn things they might otherwise have missed. Here are two students' comments on their 1990 government course evaluations:

I believe the way you taught has helped me learn and retain more information than the traditional style, since the traditional style of teaching is so boring I tend to retain a lot less information than your style.

The environment [of the class] was helpful. If this had been a structured class it would have been dull, and not particularly valuable. I feel though that I did benefit from this class . . . The ways I learned the most were through the games, simulations, skits, etc. and especially Ibsen's *Enemy of the People*.

Serious teachers understand the concepts that Postman identified in a quote above about children learning when they are interested in what they learn and "that reason is best cultivated when it is rooted in robust emotional ground." Teachers do need to find ways of tapping the interest of kids, of getting them involved, of motivating them. Clearly many educational philosophers, not just John Dewey and Jean Jacques Rousseau, have understood motivation, have understood that there is a link between reason and emotion. As Postman indicates, one often needs to use the latter to cultivate the former. Even very bright, academically motivated students need a link between reason and emotion—need to become involved in what they are asked to learn. Sean, a 1987 South Lakes graduate quoted earlier, and who is very motivated and bright, said this in his alumni survey response about the use of these kinds of activities:

My pleasant [academic] memories [of high school] include reading a book called *Flatland* in 9th grade geometry, helping construct a model medieval city in 9th grade world civilization class, doing a science fair project about a famous physics experiment for 10th grade chemistry (and getting incorrect results), producing a videotaped report about Salvador Dali for 11th grade Spanish and participating in a reader's theater production of Ibsen's *Enemy of the People* for 12th grade government. My least pleasant memories include the endless lists of vocabulary words for English classes, memorizing poems for Russian classes, labeling pictures of human bodies with appropriate anatomical names for biology, and reading textbooks for history.

You may notice a trend here. The academic things I enjoyed in high school were unusual, whereas the things I didn't enjoy were monotonous. When I say "unusual" I mean I was doing something for a course that I would not expect to do for that course, like constructing a city for a social studies course, reading a book for a math course, learning about art in a Spanish course, producing a Norwegian play for an American government course . . . the unusual projects sure were . . . interesting. They also made us pull together knowledge from a range of subjects. For instance, the reader's theater production of *Enemy of the People* allowed me to remember some of what I had learned in 11th grade about Arthur Miller's writing style. [The version of Ibsen's play used in class was a Miller adaptation.]

TV changed the "emotional ground"

The need for motivational activities is primarily because attending school is involuntary, not because of the competition presented by TV. A student who is already interested in learning something does not need external motivation. On the other hand, television has been the major factor in radically changing the "emotional ground" on which the modern teacher tries to entice students to learn. This is to a great extent because television has radically changed the way we take in and give out information altogether, as Postman amply documents in his book.

Specifically, as he says, TV has made the traditional methods of teaching and learning—lectures and book-reading—much less effective if not outright obsolete. It is no cliche to say that by and large kids do resist reading today more than they did even 30 years ago, before television became as dominant as it is now. Tolerance for straight lectures, though maybe never as high as the lecturer would have liked, has become virtually nil among high school kids. While other factors help to account for the resistance to reading and lecturing, more than anything else, television is the main cause.

Television has provided for kids a type of activity that is far more dramatic than virtually anything that can be done in the classroom. Today's students are barely conscious of the way TV has affected them, since it always has been with them. TV has become so pervasive in our lives that it has set the norm in the minds of most students for what learning is all about. It is virtually impossible for any other medium to compete with TV. Indeed, television in a sense has set the norm for life itself. This idea was exquisitely captured in the 1970 cartoon from *The New Yorker* shown on the next page.

The ante has been raised for getting kids involved. To be effective, activities have to come as close as possible to simulating TV in pace and drama—and in a classroom it usually is not possible to come very close. This means teachers must fill in the gaps either with their own personalities (be as entertaining as they can be) or with motivational activities. Otherwise, the kids still have to be persuaded in some other way to take the lesson at hand seriously, and complain that they are bored and don't like the class —"It's no fun!" In fact, kids often *are* bored, partly because the teacher may present material in a boring way but also because they have become conditioned by TV to expect learning to be entertainment—to be like Sesame Street, as Postman notes.

Postman reminds us that:

> . . . [E]ducation philosophers have assumed that becoming acculturated is difficult because it necessarily involves the imposition of restraints . . . that there must be a sequence to learning, that perseverance and a certain measure of perspiration are indispensable . . . that learning to be critical and to think conceptually and rigorously do not come easily to the young but are hard-fought victories.[9]

And then he adds the bad news: that TV provides what appears to be a way out of all this restraint and hard work, "a delicious alternative," in his wonderful phrase.[10]

"Don't you understand? This is life, this is what is happening. We can't switch to another channel."

Media hype

The central problem of TV is its very existence and the fact that virtually everything on it must be packaged as entertainment. This is exacerbated by the basic style of TV that has developed over the past 40 years: most programming is presented at fever pitch. Almost everything that is presented is done in such a way as to bamboozle people, to excite, to cloud the mind, to coerce. Almost everything on TV is hype—media hype. TV screams at the audience. Almost everything is run at a very fast pace. Images are flashed rapidly with melodramatic, loud music or loud voices in the background. There is rarely allowance for pause or reflection, as Postman says. This approach is perhaps most obvious in ads, but it is not only in ads.[11] And while media hype may be less pronounced on public TV, it is there, too—more so than ever now that public TV has become big business trying to compete with the commercial networks and cable TV.

So it is harder than ever for students to be patient with the complexities and the hard work of serious learning, especially learning abstract concepts and ideas. TV has radically changed the way we take in and give out information.

Media hype's message is that programs must get across any points or ideas as simply and quickly as possible. Complexities, subtleties, uncertainties just aren't there. The implication when teaching kids in school is that if the subject matter cannot be reduced quickly to the TV-level mentality, that subject or lesson becomes boring. Kids resist complex learning more than ever, especially learning by the traditional methods of lecturing and textbook reading.[12] They just tune out. Threats of receiving poor grades don't work, especially for kids who are seen as academically weak students. Some students will "learn" the lesson, but only long enough to pass a test and get a grade—in reality they will have genuinely learned little.

So, while the job of the teacher remains what it always was—to help kids learn and grow—TV has made this job more difficult. Media hype is a pervasive influence that increases the resistance many students already have to serious learning. Now kids must also be helped to get past the seductive clutches of TV. This is not easy, though it *can* be done. Kids are willing. Given a genuine opportunity to learn and strong encouragement by a teacher who has developed good rapport with them, even students who are generally seen as academically poor will tackle serious, complex issues.

Glued to the tube

But the interesting irony about TV is that while its chief characteristic is hype, it also tends to mesmerize. It induces passivity. Television requires virtually no investment of effort by the viewer. With attendance at movies in a theater, at least one has to leave the house. With a remote control for the tube, one does not even have to leave a chair. It is no accident that the term "couch potato" has come into our lexicon.

One by-product of this is that the natural curiosity of youth, already wounded by school, is wounded further by being conditioned to the idea that one can "learn" by doing nothing more than watch television. And of course this is on top of what is often an initial natural resistance to learning abstract concepts and ideas.

The mesmerizing effect of TV decreases student willingness to grapple with complex issues. Young people are told they must perform this unpleasant task over a 12-year period of their first 18 years, in a school building set apart from the rest of life. And all this time they are told that these are the best years of their lives, that being young is wonderful. They are courted as a distinct group by advertisers. They are seduced into buying products ad infinitum that define their status as youth and teenagers. Who is the seducer?—TV.

Other media—newspapers, magazines, radio, movies—engage in hype and deception also. Many newspapers used to be even more deceptive than they are now. But when it comes to the ability to influence values and behavior, radio and the print media pale next to TV. The hype factor has been massively increased by television. Motion pictures, which certainly have had an enormous impact on American lives, and before TV were perhaps the primary medium for defining our popular culture (and exporting it overseas), are nowhere near as influential as TV.[13]

Sound bites

During recent political campaigns we became more aware than ever of a significant refinement in the use of television to reduce issues and ideas to slogans. The term "sound bite" both describes the refinement and is a symbol of the way TV provides the "delicious alternative" to thinking. Complex issues of race, environment, education and foreign policy are often presented in 30-second, sophisticated advertisements. Why should students bother to do more when experts can deal with difficult issues so neatly and sway opinion so easily? In a modern version of the Brutus and Anthony speeches at Caesar's funeral in Shakespeare's *Julius Caesar*, polls indicate significant shifts in opinion after every set of sound bites. If political leaders can be elected in this way, with serious dialogue and debate reduced to sound bites, then why expect that TV-addicted students should be interested in grappling with serious, complex issues in school? A hopeful sign may be the increased serious discussion of ideas in the 1992 presidential campaign. If this keeps up, it should help encourage students to grapple seriously with ideas.

In addition to television's characteristic of presenting virtually all visual images very rapidly, with little or no time for reflection, TV programs are very loud. Many people, but especially young people, subject themselves to very loud talk and music, and visual images coming at them with machine gun rapidity. How does complex, contemplative learning compete with a steady diet of rapid images and excessive volume? And if it is true that TV has made it more difficult to get even academically-gifted students to take complex learning seriously, then this must be thoroughly explored and dealt with by schools as well as by parents.

Thus, television has affected the nature of learning in many ways:

- It has become superimposed on an already existing need to devise motivational activities/gimmicks for students who are involuntarily in school.
- It heightens the "need" for more dramatic, faster-paced gimmicks.
- It tends to mesmerize viewers, inducing a passivity that leads to students avoiding becoming involved with learning because to get involved requires an effort that TV has demonstrated is not necessary.
- It increases the impatience with learning anything that students do not want to learn—especially abstract concepts whose purpose is not immediately understood
- It makes it harder than ever to teach via traditional methods of reading assignments and straight lectures.
- It increases resistance to wrestling with ideas and almost eliminates the need to think by conditioning viewers to see complex issues and facts in oversimplified, thus often distorted, ways.

It's here to stay

Television is dangerous. But it is not going away. It is here to stay. Postman is right when he labels as "straight Luddite" calls for eliminating television.[14] Such positions deflect us from the job of learning how to neutralize the bad effects of TV and to convert the medium to some advantage. This is true for any technology. Once it is a part of us, it stays with us. The job becomes to use it well, to control it so it does not control us.

Postman obviously is concerned about this also. He says:

> The problem . . . does not reside in *what* we watch. The problem is *that* we watch. The solution must be found in *how* we watch [emphases his].

He does not have a complete solution in part because, as he says, "[W]e have yet to learn what television is, . . ." But he suggests a deceptively simple approach to the solution, one that schools could be central to, if they only would: many questions about TV and about information must be asked. He says that to learn what television truly is we must understand "what information is and how it gives direction to a culture."[15]

Quoting former Federal Communications Commissioner Nicholas Johnson, "Americans [should] begin talking back to their television sets," Postman adds, "For no medium is excessively dangerous if its users understand what its dangers are. It is not important that those who ask the questions arrive at" any particular set of answers. "This is an instance in which the asking of the questions is sufficient."[16]

Postman is not overly hopeful about the role of the schools in achieving what he calls "media consciousness" as a vehicle for gaining some control over television. ". . . the conventional American solution to all dangerous social problems . . . is . . . a naive and mystical faith in the efficacy of education. The process rarely works. In the matter at hand, there is even less reason than usual to expect it to. Our schools have not yet even got around to examining the role of the printed word in our culture."[17]

At the same time, Postman seems to acknowledge that we do not have a lot of choice but to use the schools, given the nature of our society. "And yet there is reason to suppose that the situation is not hopeless. Educators are not unaware of the effects of television on their students . . . they have become somewhat 'media conscious'."[18]

Many teachers accept TV

Educators may have become more media conscious, but they have not seriously addressed the impact of TV, let alone how to control it—how to counter its impact on students and learning. There is not a great understanding of the kinds of issues Postman raises. Indeed, teachers rarely even mention them. Conversations with new teachers and student teachers make it clear that even in current teacher education courses there is little dialogue about the impact of TV. One new, young teacher recently suggested that part of the reason is that those in teacher training and many of their trainers are of the generation that grew up with TV and accept it as a matter of course. They may see it as harmful because of a lack of quality or an excess of quantity but not just because of its existence.

Another major reason why TV's impact and how to control it are not being dealt with by the schools has to do with a central theme of this book: teaching students how to ask key questions, and encouraging them to do so, is not strongly rooted in our public schools. Too many teachers and administrators play it safe. Too many are Authower —and by its nature, Authower does not encourage students to raise questions that might threaten the authority and power of the one in control. Partly because of the Authower syndrome schools tend to encourage students to conserve and pigeon-hole knowledge, not to liberate and explore new knowledge. There is great resistance to doing anything new and, as Postman says, "to ask of our schools that they engage in the task of demythologizing media is to ask something the schools have never done."[19] Indeed, schools should not only be leading the process of demythologizing media, but demythologizing all enterprises that have power over people. But this, too, is asking schools to do something they have never done, and are unlikely to do without major changes.

The matter is not hopeless, but it is an uphill fight. Teachers *are* more media conscious than ever, at some level of consciousness. They certainly are aware that TV has a great impact on their students, even if there seems to be little understanding of exactly how that impact manifests itself or what can be done about it. Or, as Postman puts it, educators' "consciousness centers on the question, How can we use television (or the computer, or word processor) to control education? They have not yet got to the question, How can we use education to control television (or the computer, or word processor)?"[20]

The consciousness level is not much different from what it was in 1985 when Postman published his book. But there are signs of movement, particularly regarding the computer, which has invaded the schools in force in the last few years. Many schools are using computers in such academic areas as the teaching of writing, spelling, physics and math, for example. As with TV, understanding computers and how to use education to control them is still a long way off, though perhaps a beginning is underway.

However, it *is* possible to teach students to ask many questions about television. Here is what Tom, a 1989 graduate of South Lakes High School, said in his alumni survey response about questioning and TV:

> I do think that your class was an essential part of the preparation [for college]. You *made* us face reality. [Tom's emphasis] . . . to tell us that we must learn to listen, make decisions, and think. *I no longer live in TV land*, [my emphasis] and I face the homeless, the hungry, pollution, violence, the world everyday. It's very scary, but I know that I'm armed and ready to fight for what I believe.

Video tapes are not quite the same

Other than encouraging students not to watch so much TV, there is not a lot schools can do to stop or limit home watching of it. However, there are some things teachers can do at school to at least somewhat control TV. One, as Postman suggests, is to encourage students to ask many questions about TV. A second thing teachers can do is to make more effective use of video tape cassettes. These are common in schools but teachers do not necessarily use them effectively. Most of the time videos serve as a baby-sitter either for use by a sub or by the teacher while he or she is doing some paper work. Or tapes are used as the television itself is used: just played as one would a regular TV show.

But they can be more useful than straight TV. Above all, what makes video tapes different from straight TV is that one can control tapes. One can edit them. One can fast-forward them. One can stop showing a tape at any point to discuss it or to answer students' questions. In a sense, a video tape is not unlike a book: one can go back and re-view something, as one can go back and re-read something in a book. (A crucial difference between a tape and a book is that with a tape one cannot do the equivalent of underlining key passages—at least not with available technology.)

A video tape is not as intellectually valid or useful as a book. Like television itself, by its nature a video tape is primarily entertainment. But it *is* more useful than straight TV. And video tapes can stimulate interest in a subject quite effectively. They can be examined in a clinical way. If a teacher does ask the kinds of questions Postman suggests, does encourage students to do likewise, and does use tapes judiciously (in a limited way for information or motivation), then they offer one avenue toward education controlling TV. It is only a start, but it is better than impotently lamenting TV while it continues to do its damage.

As a high school teacher I saw vividly the impact of television (and other technology). I hope that eventually education will be used to control it. However, this will require changing the system drastically. And the system has always resisted fundamental change. The ultimate way to control TV is to bring a far greater measure of reality to education, and to create a we/we, inviting school environment that gets kids so involved with learning—and life—that the "need" for TV will recede. In this case, television can be what it is best at: entertainment—no more dangerous, ideally, than any movie in a theater.

Notes

1. Viking Books, 1985
2. So valuable did I find the book that I bought several copies and started a special lending library for fellow teachers I could get to read it. Having discussed many of the book's ideas with my students, I also lent the book to several of them and had a few who wrote reports about the book or reports using the book as a major resource.
3. An exception may be C-Span, which to a remarkable degree manages to provide programming that is as free from being entertainment packaging as I think it is possible to get on TV.
4. Ibid.,pages   159–160
5. Ibid., Page 90
6. Ibid., Page 146
7. Ibid., Page 144
8. Ibid., Page 154. Yet the temptation to entertain kids to get them to learn is powerful. When Postman says that "students will not rebel . . . if their social studies teacher sings to them the facts about the War of 1812" [Page 156], I want to laugh and cry at once. I sometimes did virtually just that sort of thing! And when I did it, I felt keenly the dilemma: how much of this was helping the kids learn the substance of whatever I was being funny or entertaining about, and how much became mainly entertainment while they were in my class?
9. Ibid., page 146
10. Ibid.,page 147
11. It has always struck me as fascinating that many people who regularly watch commercial TV say that the best thing on TV generally are the ads. Why not? As pure entertainment they have become very sophisticated. That they also brainwash is another matter.
12. Oversimplification and distortion of knowledge did not start with TV, of course. Textbooks have always generally oversimplified allegedly to make material more palatable to the reader. In the course of doing this, the material has quite often been distorted.
13. Movies cannot be as powerful in determining behavior, even though before the com-

petition from TV movies were a powerful determinant. Since one must make a conscious decision to go to a theater, it does require at least some effort to be influenced by movies. But TV watching is virtually effortless and can almost be done unconsciously. I do not know if there is data about how many people turn on the set just to see what's on without having in mind a particular program they wish to see, which would be an index of conscious-ness or not about TV, but I'll bet the number is high. Equally, I would bet there is a large number of people who keep the TV on almost continuously, somewhat like many people do a radio—sort of like background music. Surely the values and behavior of people in these categories are open to being influenced by TV even more than people who consciously turn on the set to see a particular program and then turn it off.

14. Ibid., page 158
15. Ibid.
16. Ibid., Page 161
17. Ibid.,page 162
18. Ibid., Page 162
19. Ibid. I do not agree with Postman that educators—anyway, public high school teachers in general—"are apt to find new methods congenial, especially if they are told that education can be accomplished more efficiently by means of the new techniques." [p. 143] If a new technique requires too much change in the current routines, or requires lots of thought and work to implement, or is too threatening, then my experience is that most high school teachers will strongly resist the new technique.
20. Ibid., Page 162–63

The Answers:
Beating the Game

13

The System as It Is: A Temporary Fix

There is very little chance of any significant movement toward good education within the system as it is. There are three main reasons.

The System is entrenched

Essentially, the structure and assumptions of American public high schools are the same at the approach of the the turn of the 21st century as they were in 1900. Yet, in virtually every way imaginable the world is a very different place today from what it was then. Politically, sociologically, economically, scientifically, medically, psychologically, technologically—the world has changed tremendously in the last hundred years. But the public high school is essentially the same. It is similar to what Albert Einstein said about the advent of the atomic bomb: that its invention changed everything but our way of thinking. Parents and the general public are used to the schools as they are, even while sometimes complaining about them. This partly reflects the fact that there is no general agreement about what education should be, but a set of assumptions that have evolved over the years. The educational system is a multi-billion dollar industry, directly and indirectly providing jobs and income for millions of teachers, administrators, maintenance and clerical workers, teacher training colleges, textbook writers and publishers. It is big business. It can be political dynamite. The thought of radically changing it is frightening, both for the general public that supports the system with its taxes and for those whose livelihoods depend on it. This is especially so since kids do seem to get an education, inadequate as it may be.

Educators are not trained to function in a we/we, non-Authower kind of environment.

Even in teacher training colleges that try to acquaint prospective

155

teachers and administrators with non-traditional approaches to education, the assumption is that they will be teaching in schools which are essentially we/they and Authower run. By and large, prospective educators are trained to function in these kinds of schools.

The System itself strongly re-enforces this assumption.

Teachers and administrators who start their careers with non-traditional ideas about how they and the school should function quickly learn that they are swimming upstream. The system rewards conformity and compliance, not creativity and questioning. It takes unusual teachers or administrators to continue battling during their entire careers. Those who resist to begin with, eventually cave in and become part of the system.

Of course, just because an institution is old doesn't mean it is of no value in a changing world. That venerable 18th century document, the U.S. Constitution, still works quite well for a very different 20th century. But it was designed to be flexible. Its words are open to interpretation in light of changing circumstances and it can be formally amended. But the school system is inflexible; it does not lend itself to formal or informal change. At best it lends itself to tinkering.

Nothing new

Most adults walking into a public high school today would recognize what is going on as similar to their own experience.

And what is going on, by and large, is an uninvolving, not very intellectually challenging, non-nurturing, frequently confrontational, teacher-directed and involuntary experience for young people.

Adults entering most high schools today would see the same structure of periods, requirements, tests and student behavior that existed when they were in high school. And the we/they environment with Authower enshrined, exists now as then, though sometimes with a softer face than in days past. Schools have learned how to screen the abuse of authority and power behind a wall of pleasant-sounding rhetoric. Parents are not as likely to hear from a teacher or administrator, "Mrs. Pirt, your son is a trouble-maker. He must change or get out." Parents are more likely to hear, "Your son is having trouble adjusting to school this year. We really need to work on his behavior or find some alternative way of educating him." But in the end it all comes out the same: "Mrs. Pirt, we would rather not have your son in this school."

The eleven-point program

Not much can be done in any fundamental sense to truly improve high schools. But there are things that could be done to mitigate the damage they now do.

This is my eleven-point program for improvement:

1. Take the feelings of kids seriously.

What is important to them may seem trivial or wrong-headed to adults. But if the adults truly want to reach the kids and help them, if the adults want to steer kids in directions their experience tells them are beneficial, then first they must establish genuine rapport with the kids. Essential to this process is taking the kids seriously.

2. Let students in on what is happening and why.

Lift the veil of mystery that keeps kids—and parents—from understanding how the school, how the teacher, operates. Whether the matter is an individual teacher's assignment or an administrator's ruling about some conflict, the kids must know fully and accurately why something is happening that affects them. And, students must be allowed to participate honestly in decision-making about issues that affect them.

3. Give students real, meaningful work and responsibilities.

Eliminate busywork assignments—and where such assignments are absolutely necessary, make *very* sure that the students understand why.

Encourage students to explore things for themselves. Even in a framework set by the teacher or by some requirement of the system, by far the best way for high school-age kids to learn is to be put in a situation where they must find out for themselves. Assignments should force them to explore and get to the point where they must ask questions and want to do so. In other words, make self-direction an integral part of the classroom experience for all students. Minimize requiring that students read (memorize) the textbook and then regurgitate that back on a test. There are better ways to learn any subject. This does not mean the teacher cannot *teach*. It does mean that when the teacher teaches, students will be much more likely to learn what the teacher says, be able to integrate the teacher's information with what they learned on their own, and thus be able to make sense of it.

Encourage students to participate in individual or small group field trips, with the requirement that they write about what happened, and discuss their experiences with the class, and relate them to other things in the course and to other courses.

Since so many high school students have after school jobs or do worthwhile volunteer work, teachers should systematically give students course credit for relating their work/volunteering experiences to the course. Students could write papers or give oral presentations to the class, for example. This may not be possible for every lesson and every course, but with a little imagination, I am sure many teachers and students could see ways of relating job and volunteer activities to much of what goes on in classes. The true story of volunteering in a homeless shelter or as a candy striper in a hospital could inspire other students. And giving credit for the experience would help connect the school to the rest of the world, and would help students see that there is a value to school.

Develop involving techniques. The circle classroom seating arrangement is one way, but not the only one. Many classrooms, such as labs with stationary tables, do not lend themselves to the circle arrangement. The circle is not magic. The critical thing is for students to be engaged—to be actively, not passively, involved in what they are asked to learn.

4. Examine the effect and use of both television and video tape cassettes.

Make sure that use of videos in classes is valid—that is, that it has a useful purpose that genuinely is integral to the course of study and is not simply a baby-sitting device. Make sure students understand why they are watching what they are being asked to watch. And, as much as possible, during the same class period when a video is shown some time should be provided to discuss it, and to encourage students' questions. Just showing a video for a whole period with no discussion or questions probably means the kids will interpret the use of the video as baby-sitting and take it less seriously.[1]

5. Actively involve parents in the life of the school.

Parents need to do more than just come to the annual dog-and-pony show called Back-to-School night; more than just joining the Parent-Teacher Association [PTA]. PTAs are largely the province of middle/upper middle class parents who know how to work the system. Parents of poor kids, and of minority kids, generally feel excluded. Moreover, PTAs easily become tools of the school principal, their function frequently being public relations and fund-raising.

To actively involve parents, teachers must tell parents what is going on in their courses—via newsletters, phone calls or meetings. Teachers should be willing to meet with or talk with parents in the evenings or weekends, which may be the only time many parents can meet or talk. Parents should be encouraged to visit the school periodically to see for themselves what goes on. Parents can be mentors and tutors and sources of information—and sources of jobs. Some students will not like the idea of their parents being that involved. But as students are brought more into the process of the school, into the process of their own learning, they are likely to see involving parents as legitimate. And, where a teacher finds out that a particular family situation is such that it would be harmful for the student to have his or her parents involved, then the teacher should use discretion and act accordingly. Moreover, some parents will not have the time or interest to be involved. But at the very least they should be given a *genuine* opportunity and should be encouraged to get involved when and where they can and want to. Teachers do not need to see parents as the enemy—as part of "they" in a we/they environment. Parents, as well as students, should be seen as part of a we/we environment.

6. Eliminate the whole pass scene.

Passes demean students and teachers, are a waste of time and paper, disrupt the process of learning, and re-enforce the we/they environment.

7. Eliminate the whole grading/testing business.

Evaluation of students should be a collaborative effort between students and teachers and, where it seems necessary, parents. It should not be a game, a test to see what students can memorize and heave back, a test to see what students do not know. If our purpose in education is to help students learn and grow, then, for example, when a teacher discovers that a student does not know something, the next step should be to help that student learn what she or he did not know, not to give the student a low or failing grade and let it go at that.

In their book *Portfolio Assessment in the Reading-Writing Classroom*, Robert J. Tierney, Mark A. Carter and Laura E. Desai provide a model for evaluation that can be used in any classroom. Their premise is that students must be actively engaged in the process of evaluating their own work, and not be the objects of a grade given by a teacher after taking a test or writing a paper or doing a lab assignment. The portfolio is a place where the work of a student can be stored. But "portfolios are not objects. They are vehicles for ongoing assessment by students. They represent activities and processes . . . more than they do products."[2] These processes include selecting the material to be evaluated, comparing the quality of what a student did in one paper or report (or whatever) to something else *that same student* has done, goal-setting by the student with help from the teacher, and self-evaluation by the student. The focus is on the continual business of helping students improve their knowledge and skills, and their own understanding of these, rather than on the teacher's grade for test or paper or project. Tierney, et al, explain the Portfolio further:

> Portfolios are systematic collections [of student material] . . .
> They can serve as the basis to examine effort, improvement, pro-
> cesses, and achievement as well as to meet the accountability
> demands usually achieved by more formal testing procedures.
> Through reflection on systematic collections of students' work, teach-
> ers and students can work together to illuminate students' strengths,
> needs and progress.[3]

The authors also talk about the values involved in using portfolios.
These values include "a belief in developing procedures for planning classroom learning that represent what students are actively doing; a commitment to student involvement in self-evaluation and helping students to
become aware of their own development . . . " The authors also identify
"the values that underlie the use of portfolios" as including "a belief in
the view that assessment should take into consideration" such elements
as: (1) the processes learners use; (2) "the products they develop"; (3)
"the improvements they achieved"; and (4) "the effort they put forth."[4]

This kind of collaboration between teacher and student to evaluate
student work is quite possible in any subject, not only in the reading and
writing areas that are the special focus of Tierney's book. This process
can be adapted to any high school course.[5]

There are other evaluation methods, discussed in earlier chapters,
that, while not as satisfactory as what Tierney proposes, move in that
direction. These include self-evaluation, individual conferences and whole
class evaluations.

Another kind of assessment is the writing project, modeled on techniques developed in various school writing project programs around the
United States. The purpose is to give students experience in writing essays
in class on topics they know, and in evaluating each other's essays. In
this scenario, the students know the general topic before they start writing
but not the specific questions to be addressed in the essay. The day after
they write they meet in groups and evaluate each others' essays, using
criteria that had been developed in advance—*criteria developed in a collaborative effort between teacher and students*. Then each student selects
one of the essays written from among those completed within a grading
period for the teacher to evaluate—and grade. Though this approach is
not the wholly collaborative effort Tierney, et al, propose, it moves in
that direction. It gives students valuable writing and evaluation experience
and can be used with virtually any group of students.

A question that might be raised about eliminating testing and grades
is the matter of how to determine whether or when a student has achieved

enough credits to gain a high school diploma. The portfolio system, or an adaptation of it, does not prevent requiring that students take certain courses or a minimum number of courses. It simply means that the decision about a student's completion of a course would be made collaboratively by the student and the teacher, rather than by the teacher alone.

8. Classes must be small.

Smaller classes have been a battle cry of teachers forever. There simply is no doubt whatsoever that classes above 20 are much less conducive to serious learning. Ideally, classes should have about 15 students. There should be enough kids to allow some variety and interaction among them, yet not be too many for the teacher to be able to work with all the students individually as well as collectively.

9. Teachers should teach fewer students.

A variation of the class size problem is the total number of students most high school teachers instruct in a day. The number is somewhere between 120 and 150 for teachers of academic classes. Physical education teachers often have more than 150. Wonderful as young people are, that is simply too many people to work with everyday —especially when the teacher is trying to create a we/we environment in which honest interactive relationships with students are developed. Getting to know students well enough to be of genuine help to each of them is infinitely more difficult when working with so many young people. Many teachers simply give up trying. This is a big reason why many teachers are more comfortable in a formal, we/they environment. With too many kids in a day, it is easier to be in control if the teacher maintains distance and does not try to really develop relationships. But that also means that the students are less likely to learn and grow as they can and should. If teachers had five classes of 15 or even 20 each, the total would be 75 to 100: a more manageable number.

10. Vary the schedule of classes.

The notion that every class must meet every day at the same time is valid only in the Lego model of schools. Not all class periods always need the same length of time. Nor do courses always need to meet at the same time regularly. This is not an argument for variety for the sake of variety. Length of class periods and frequency of class meetings should relate to the nature of what is going on and not be determined by a rigid, often counterproductive pre-set schedule. Like the substance of learning and the rules of the institution, the schedule of classes should be organic, dictated by what is needed for students to learn and grow effectively, not by administrative convenience. In the computer age it should be no problem to create a more flexible schedule, especially if the rationale for doing this is the organic needs of courses.[6]

11. Student teachers/administrators must be taught self-awareness and socio-economic-political reality, using the same methods advocated for high school students, and more on-the-job training.

Authower must be attacked. Logical places are in the training of educators, by helping students and parents learn to deal with it, and by building limits into the institution's power. Teaching is a helping profession. The helpers must be as fully aware of themselves as possible—not merely aware of their talents, strengths and weaknesses, but of their flash points, the things that anger them. Some type of psychological training must be an integral part of teacher/administrative training. And the methods used should basically be the same as for teaching kids: teachers should be actively involved in the process of their training. Moreover, teachers should have ample opportunity to test out their skills—something more than just a semester of traditional student teaching, which is often an artificial, unsatisfying experience. And, teacher trainees should experience *as students* the we/we classroom.

At present, to become a teacher or an administrator one has only to pass certain courses, some of which may be useful and some not, and do student teaching which, again, may or may not be useful. Some states and school systems also now require that new teachers pass the national teacher exam, or some local equivalent. But these exams have the same flaw as do all tests: they require the test taker to spit back information she or he may or may not understand. Tests do not, cannot, ascertain whether the person will be a creative, caring teacher who engages kids and helps them learn and grow.

The central problem with current teacher training is that it does not get at the guts, the core, of those who wish to become teachers. It does not require teacher or administrator candidates to look carefully at themselves, to honestly *know* themselves. Without such self-knowledge, people are likely to feel anger and frustration they do not understand and cannot cope with effectively. Thus a teacher or administrator without self-knowledge easily becomes Authower, for Authower provides a convenient outlet on the job—and the system readily invites it. It is easy to take anger and frustration out on kids, who are vulnerable targets in the hierarchical, authoritarian, we/they environment of high schools. The only way to get at the core is for school systems to take the risk of doing much more on-the-job training of teachers. This could be set up as an apprenticeship arrangement. But the key is that prospective teachers should start working with students *at the very beginning* of their training and throughout the process.

Teacher training should also include much more understanding of the socio-economic-political forces that materially affect public education in this country. Teachers generally tend to be naive or uninformed about these forces. Some teachers may have a sense that most significant decisions about how schools are run, and what is and is not allowed by the system, are socio-economic-political decisions. Fewer teachers understand who makes the decisions or how they are made. Yet teachers need to be highly aware of these things so they can build them into the courses they teach and take can them into account in developing relationships with their students. Teachers also need to understand the socio-economic-political forces so they can cope effectively with them.

A few more quick fixes

There are other ideas for changing the system as it is. One suggestion that has been advocated in recent years, and tried out in some school systems, is school-based management. Major decisions affecting a school would be made at the school itself and not in the school district's central office. Each school would have its own budget to spend. The principal, along with other administrators and, possibly, teachers, would make the basic budgetary decisions for that school: how much should be spent on books, equipment, and other areas. And decisions about hiring and firing of staff also would be made locally. School-based management is appealing since it seems to cut down on system-wide bureaucracy and provide a way for each school to be more responsive to its own students and parents. The problem is that, by itself, school-based management does not address the core problems of the system. It cannot address the core problems *unless* it is accompanied by a process whereby the school develops a we/we environment and becomes a place in which the educational experience for young people is involving, intellectually challenging, exciting, inviting, nurturing, non-confrontational, self-directed and voluntary.

These suggestions, while not requiring a fundamental change in the structure of the system as it is, *will* require changes, and some of these will be radical. They will affect the basic philosophical premises of the system. The changes will be required of educators, students, parents and the general public.

For instance, educators will have to seriously address the unstated but very real sorting out/ranking function of schools. Citizens will have to be willing to spend more money on schools, since smaller classes will use more teachers[7] In turn, this will require an acknowledgement that it takes more money to meaningfully educate students in small classes than to sort out and rank them and superficially educate them en masse. But it will be possible to convince people to spend more money on schools if citizens can be shown the value to the *whole* society of good education.

Parents will have to take seriously the need to get actively involved in their children's education. This is not an easy thing to do for people who are busy with jobs and other activities and whose kids may not like much parental involvement in their lives. And kids will have to change focus from learning how to play games and con the system to becoming students in the many ways that are possible.

None of this will be easy, of course. Change rarely is. People resist it. But, difficult as the task may be, it is possible. *If* we are serious about the state of our schools, we *may* be able to effect at least *some* meaningful change within the system as it is.

Notes

1. I understand that if a teacher is showing a movie that lasts more than one class period, it seems necessary to use the entire period in order to show the whole film in as few days as possible. But even here, it is preferable to find some way of engaging the kids along the way in what is shown, via questions each period after that day's part of the film, or questions or comments students must bring to class the next day, or the like. Just to show a film, even a powerful, serious Great Movie, over several days without engaging the kids along the way is of questionable value, especially given the amount of TV they already watch.

2. Tierney, et al, Op. Cit., Page 41

3. Ibid.

4. Ibid.

5. Ibid., Page 48

6. Flexible scheduling has been used in a number high schools in the United States. The problem often has been that the decision to have flexible scheduling was made by the administration with teachers and students not involved in the process, with the resulting resistance that should have been expected. Even where there has been some teacher involvement, the implementation of flexible scheduling often has not been done with enough lead time or the allocation of enough support for teachers and students to help them become comfortable with it and learn to work out kinks. But done with full involvement of students, teachers and administrators, and with adequate support and time, flexible scheduling makes great sense.

7. However, as discussed in the next chapter, smaller classes in conjunction with training young people to be more self-directed will not necessarily mean more teachers.

14

A New System Altogether: The Grow/Learn System

Remember the futility of trying to add an arm to a clay figure after it has been completed? It may stick for a while, but before long it will fall off and a new solution to the armless body problem will have to be found. The system as it is reminds us of that sad figure. It can no longer be fixed by sticking new arms onto its clay body.

A radical departure

We need a radical departure from the present system. We need a totally new system of helping young people learn and grow. And *this time* the premise and the focus must be different from the system as it is. There must be a consensus about the purposes and functions of the new system.

The *premise* of a new system should be that the purpose of high school is to provide a framework and a mechanism for *all* young people to continue learning in every way possible, and to test out that learning in the world around them in order to discover paths along which they want to take their lives; ways in which they can become active, questioning and responsible citizens of this republic; and what they need to learn and do to achieve these goals.

A vital *assumption* is that useful learning and growing for young people happens in many ways and in many places. Students learn not only from teachers in classrooms during school hours, but on field trips, on jobs, on their own, from each other and from parents. This being so, the new high school must build in as many ways as possible for students to learn and grow.

The *focus* of a high school education should be on maintaining a we/we environment in which young people are *invited* to grow and learn, are *involved* in the process of their own learning and growing, are *excited* about it, are *intellectually challenged*, and are given every opportunity to practice being *self-directed* people. The focus should also be on adults *nurturing* young people and working with them in *non-confrontational* ways. In the new system *there must be a close correlation between what happens in school and in the rest of the world*, so that all students truly see the point of learning: that it is to help them find ways *they* see as useful in order to establish their places in the world and to develop their skills and interests to the maximum extent they can and want to. Thus learning becomes *voluntary*, because it makes sense.

All this is very different from the premise, assumption and focus of the system as it is. It is different from sorting and ranking students, different from "covering the curriculum" regardless of its value or use, different from assuming that all learning and growing comes from a teacher in a classroom, different from covertly and overtly imposing on kids requirements and constraints whose purposes are difficult to see, different from isolating school and young people from the rest of society. In short, this new system is different because it is involving, intellectually stimulating, exciting, inviting, nurturing, non-confrontational, self-directed and voluntary.

Of course, the educational system must make clear to young people what are the norms and values of the society it reflects. It has an obligation to make clear to young people what are society's expectations of them, and that there are consequences of actions. Kids *do* want to know these things. But they also want and need an opportunity to explore these matters for themselves. Young people need to discover for themselves the many variations of our society's norms, values and expectations, so that they may decide how and where they fit in to the scheme of things. They have to be able to decide in what ways they may develop their own variations on the norms and values.

The main components

Here, then, are the main components of a high school based on the Grow/Learn System:

Student self-direction training.

When students first enroll in this high school, they receive training in self-direction—that is, training in how to begin the process of taking responsibility for their own learning and growth, and responsibility for their own actions. The idea of learning to be responsible for one's actions is not punitive; part of becoming a self-directed person is to understand and learn to deal with consequences of actions. The exact content and duration of the initial training depends on each student's prior experience. Younger students generally need more help and support in learning how to function in a self-directed way than do older students. But the goal is to help all students understand the value and use of self-direction. A part of the self-direction training is for students to learn about the obligations and responsibilities they have in order to complete the work for a diploma. They also learn at this time what obligations the school has to them. Students are given time and help to try out self-direction, and become comfortable with it.

Adult training.

Teachers, administrators and other adults who routinely work with students also receive training in self-direction to help them learn to use their own experiences and judgements in responding to institutional directives. Teachers in the new high school must avoid the kind of mindless waiting to be told what to do that was described in chapter seven—and is very common among teachers in the system as it is. This training also helps teachers understand and support the need for students to be as self-directed as possible. As with the students' training, the content and duration of the adults' self-direction training will depend on their prior experience and training. And they, too, will learn about their responsibilities and obligations to the students and what the students' responsibilities and obligations are to them. Of course, it is understood that the teachers already have the requisite knowledge of their subject area to be effective resources for the students.

Adults also receive training in working with students in nurturing, non-confrontational ways and, again depending on the prior experience and training the adult has, self-awareness training.

Diploma requirements.

The high school awards a diploma for having completed certain courses and other experiences. Courses the school offers are in such traditional subject areas as science, social studies, math, English, fine and performing arts, foreign languages, physical education, and vocational courses such as auto mechanics, electronics, and home economics. Other subjects may be added. "Other experiences" might be a paid or a volunteer job, or an apprenticeship. Since as a part of the program leading to the diploma students are required to have some kind of paid or unpaid work experience, courses in today's vocational education are, in this approach to high school, open to *all* students, not only those in a particular vocational program. Students also are invited to participate in sports and clubs, but this does not affect the granting of the diploma.

It is important to elaborate on the *work experience requirement*. In the current system, some high school teachers do include some kind of work or volunteer experience as one way for students to complete a particular course requirement. I required this for a senior course at Yellow Springs High School in the early 1970's. Poli Obs, described in chapter six, is an example of a different kind of non-classroom way of fulfilling a course requirement. A requirement for a work or volunteering experience of some kind is now being considered in several school systems around the country, and has been adopted by a few. But what I am suggesting goes beyond this. The model for the Grow/Learn System is the co-op program at Antioch College in Yellow Springs, Ohio, in which students alternate quarters on and off campus: on campus one quarter they do academic work, off campus another quarter they have full-time jobs. Having that exact system at the high school level may or may not be possible. But adapting the *concept* to the high school level is possible and very desirable. The central point is that academic work and jobs should be an integral part of the high school students' experiences so that they connect with the world at large and see their place in it and relationships between academic learning and the rest of life.

Teacher-mentors.

When each student enrolls in the school, she or he is assigned a teacher-mentor, a personal counselor and helper for students. The teacher-mentor helps them develop a program of classes and work experiences that, when successfully completed, will lead to the diploma. The mentor also periodically reviews with students their overall progress toward completing work for the diploma, helps students make whatever changes in their programs may be necessary, and is an adult to whom students can come for general help and guidance.

The teacher-mentor role is different from that of the counselor in the system as it is. For one thing, partly because mentors assist fewer students than do counselors, they are more accessible to students. And, the philosophical basis for the mentor-student relationship is different from that of counselor-student. The counselor in the current system helps students figure out their schedules and sometimes helps in conflicts with teachers and with other problems the students may have. But though some counselors see themselves as advocates for the kids, the system sees the counselor as its advocate—to help the kid adjust to the system. The mentor, on the other hand, is trained to take seriously what the student wants, and, consistent with the self-direction theme of the school, the mentor encourages the students to develop their own ideas for taking academic courses and for seeking work experiences within the broad framework of the diploma requirements. Moreover, in the Grow/Learn System, the mentor is supported in her or his role as a *guide* for students, someone who is there for the kids primarily, not a go-between the system and the student.

If, after the initial contacts with the teacher-mentor, the student is dissatisfied with the relationship, she or he may try to find another mentor, provided the new mentor has not reached the suggested work-load limit which would undermine the mentor's effectiveness.

The mentor, also, may seek to have a student transferred to another mentor if he or she feels the relationship is not working out. This is important so adults have some flexibility in the role. It is also important that students who are learning responsibility, and testing out the reality of the world, experience and learn to deal with problems others may be having with them as well as vice-versa.

It is recommended that, if at all possible, a third party be called in to meet with a mentor and student who are having a conflict to try to work out the relationship, using mediation techniques. The aim is that, at the very least, the relationship between student and mentor be as useful to the student as it can be, even if it is not completely desirable. It should also be at least an acceptable relationship to the mentor.

Class schedules and other activities.

Classes are not scheduled every day at the same time, but rather two or three times a week for different lengths of time, depending on the course. This is to provide time for students *within their school /work day* for other activities: field trips, doing research in the library or elsewhere, jobs, apprenticeships, volunteering with some organization, studying at home or somewhere at school, meeting with other students or with a teacher or with someone giving the student information, or participating in a school activity (a sport, a club, or what-have-you). The possibilities are almost limitless. It is up to the student to determine his or her day, within the broad program worked out with the teacher-mentor.

The "school/work day" refers to the combined hours a student spends at school and on a job or doing any other activity related to the school program. The length of each day, and where it is spent, varies with each student. The point of the term is to underscore that how much time a student spends in a particular place (classes, job, library, etc.) is determined by the nature of the task to be accomplished, not by a rigid, universal schedule.

Class sizes and teacher work-load.

In this high school, class sizes are designed to maximize the learning that goes on in the classroom, so classes have 15 to 20 students. Teachers have a maximum of four classes a day, and there is a limit on the number of students for whom they are mentors. The details are worked out at each school with the parties involved. The point is that teachers, properly trained, should also be properly supported by the school, so that their energies are used wisely and not unnecessarily drained.

Evaluation of student work.

Both academic and job experiences completed by students for fulfilling the requirements for the diploma are evaluated by using adaptations of the collaborative evaluation process discussed in the previous chapter.

Transportation.

Buses are available for students going on field trips. Mini buses also are available for taking small groups of students on field trips or job experiences if they do not have other means of transportation.

Adult roles.

While the teachers, counselors, librarians, and administrators play roles in this high school similar to those in the current system's high school, they are trained to maintain a non-confrontational, collaborative, nurturing, non-Authower, we/we relationship with students. And the Grow/Learn System supports this relationship. More than anything else, what produces this we/we environment is the behavior of the adults with the students. For example, an administrator whose basis for handling a conflict between a student and a teacher is we/we, non-confrontational, collaborative and non-Authower, is much more likely to be effective and produce less anger in the participants to the dispute than is an administrator who handles the conflict on a we/they, confrontational, Authower basis.

Financing the Grow/Learn System

There has been no study about the relative cost of the Grow/ Learn System versus the system as it is. However, the amount of money spent on education, and what it is spent for, are not written in concrete. The same unquestioned assumptions that have developed about the purpose of schools also exist about how much money is spent on schools, and for what. We are free to spend money for education any way we want to.

In some ways, the new system would seem to be more expensive, with its smaller classes and teacher loads, and its buses for field trips. However, since a great deal more student learning in the new system high school will be done without direct teacher supervision, it may be that, in the end, costs for teachers will be no more than at present. Although class sizes and teacher work-loads will be decreased in the new system, which might indicate a need for more teachers, many aspects of student learning and growth that today are supposed to happen in traditional classes would, in the Grow/Learn System, happen in other ways—such as students self-directing more of their own learning and growth in independent study and on jobs. There will be fewer group classes in the new system.

Moreover, money can be used differently from the way it is used now. For example, less money would be spent in the Grow/ Learn System on large school buildings built with the assumption that all learning for kids happens in classrooms. What is needed are smaller buildings that have some classrooms and science labs, yes, but also meeting places for kids and, as at present, some place for students to leave their belongings while participating in various activities. These buildings would be made with lighter, cheaper but sturdy material—using perhaps a geodesic design, or the like. In other words, if we accept that learning and growing for students comes in all kinds of ways and places, then school buildings can be built with more limited and more flexible purposes in mind. And the money saved could be spent on other things—such as better salaries, books, buses, and so forth.

How much will we pay?

Of course, the real question is, how much money is this society willing to pay for education? While spending for public schools is usually the biggest slice of local government budgets, as a country we still spend far less on education than we can afford to or than we should spend. Although a significant amount of school money comes these days from the state and national governments, the bulk still comes from local funds. And, to make matters worse, the main source of local funds is the anti-quated property tax, which, like the sales tax, is regressive. One index of a strong societal commitment to public education will be to raise tax money from a genuine progressive income tax—the only fair tax because it is based on the ability to pay.

More to come

More planning is necessary to bring about this new system. Others must offer suggestions to build and improve on these proposals. Indeed, it is important that many people be involved in a process of devising a new system. If one single individual tried to create by himself an entire system of education, with all the necessary details, it would be suspect. To have an educational system that works we must engage in a sustained, no-holds barred dialogue about what we mean by good education. The ideas of as many people as possible should be used in a process that eventually creates a meaningful, useful educational system for all students.

The new system described here is not going to be everyone's cup of tea. Nor, for that matter, is the definition of good education, which forms the philosophical framework for my Grow/Learn System, universally accepted. Nonetheless, it is imperative that a radical departure be made from the system as it is. What I am suggesting may seem crazy to some people just because it has a premise, assumption and focus that are entirely different from the current system. Well, I think *that* system is crazy, as I have demonstrated in this book.

There are many details about a new system that must be worked out. Most of these are technical, having to do with precise arrangements, specific diploma requirements, how students get their work experiences, keeping effective records of the various student activities and co-ordinating everything for each kid and for the whole school. It is all very possible *if we want to do this*. Administrative hassles and technical details in no way have to interfere with implementing good ideas. If they do, it is almost always because someone with power (Authower?) does not want the new idea implemented in the first place and is using technical or administrative problems as an excuse to stop it from working.

There is, however, one particular detail of the new system that I want to discuss briefly: the matter of mandatory requirements. Requirements can be positive tools *if* they make sense, are organically related to clearly stated goals, are fully understood by everyone, and allow the kids to make genuine choices in order to check out what works for them. In other words, the requirements are there because the adults' experience and perspective cause them to say to young people: there are things you need to know about and learn about that you may not yet see but will in time. This is all right *if* the requirements are enforced with compassion and wisdom and with the adults' eye on what is best for the kids, not what is best for administrative convenience. If the requirements become ends in themselves and not means for each student to grow and learn to his or her fullest, then they lose their function and we are back to square one with the system as it is. In an inviting, we/we school environment, students will be able to accept valid requirements.

Clearly this radical departure will have a major impact on the rest of society. It will especially necessitate some changes in the economic structure in order to accommodate high school students in the job market in larger numbers than in the after-school/summer mode that accounts for most current student jobs. Though many of these jobs will be part-time, a large number of the students may be working or doing apprenticeships or volunteering during the usual work day.

This won't happen easily or quickly. Students in the work force conjure up legitimate fears of child labor and of displacing adults who need jobs to support families. Certainly I am not suggesting we return to the days of children in sweatshops or coal mines. And no adult worker should be displaced. Nor is either of these a necessary consequence of this proposal. If workers and employers are involved in the process of developing a new system, part of that process will be to find ways of helping young people connect with the world beyond school to explore links between that world and the academic school world. Some will resist the kinds of changes outlined here, and others will see them as a great opportunity. But as we move into a technologically advanced, computer-driven, service-dominated economy, with so many changes in the offing that we can only dimly see them now, this is the perfect time to radically change the schools along these lines. The Grow/Learn System is an attempt to think in radically new ways to meet the need to replace the current school system and to meet the challenges of the 21st century. This is consistent with the thrust of the Clinton Administration's efforts to look at how we prepare youth for the future, how we build and rebuild our economy and our society in the global, technological world of tomorrow.

There are two potential dangers in the new system that must be mentioned here:

• Any organization or system, no matter how noble in purpose and design, has the potential for becoming rigid and self-serving, no longer fulfilling its original promise. Even if my Grow/Learn System comes to pass, the great worry is that in time it will become another system as rigid as the present one. "Who says organization says oligarchy," warned the Swiss political scientist Robert Michels, who analyzed this problem in his 1915 book, *Political Parties: A Sociological Study of the Oligarchical Tendencies of Modern Democracy*.[1]

Even in democratic institutions if those in power are not continuously held accountable to those who put them in power and to those they serve, there is a danger of their becoming self-serving or oligarchic. That danger must be acknowledged up front in order that it can be combated. There are no quick answers other than that power should be spread out in any organization so that no one person or group can completely control things. John Kenneth Galbraith addresses this with his concept of "countervailing power." The framers of the U.S. Constitution understood this and tried to set up a government of divided powers. James Madison discussed this in his famous Federalist Paper #10. In spite of public schools theoretically being controlled by citizens through a school board, real power rests mostly with an administrative hierarchy that usually manages to co-opt the school board and, quite often, the teacher organizations also—and thus be impervious to serious challenges to its entrenched system. So, to a considerable degree, the school system has become an undemocratic if not oligarchic institution. This trap must be avoided in the Grow/ Learn System. That is the reason for this warning.

● The second danger is anti-intellectualism. A high school based on the Grow/ Learn System must not become a center for anti-intellectualism, true to such a very large extent in the system as it is. The emphasis on the importance of students having work as well as academic experiences might be seen as undermining the role of schools to help students develop their minds. However, there is no need for conflict between academic/intellectual pursuit and connecting with the rest of the world partly through work. Far more intellectual challenging of students is both necessary and very possible. Connecting students with the rest of the world will help this process, especially for those students who resist academic pursuit. They need to see that developing their intellectual capacities increases their ability to function effectively in the larger world.

Ancient rabbis and medieval monks were able to exist on two levels, as laborers and scholars. And students need to learn the connection between the rest of the world and academic pursuit. Indeed, most of them want to experience the connection while they are still in school. What is needed, then, is to galvanize enough people, who see that it is in their interest and in the interest of the country, to provide this opportunity for students by creating a whole new and more useful school system.

Notes

1. 1949 Reprint by The Free Press, Glencoe, Ill; "The iron law of oligarchy," Chapter II, Part Six.

Afterword

My former students must have the last word. Obviously, I love students and think we under-challenge and infantilize them. When I remember that students in medieval Italy, who were about high school-age and a bit older, sought out teachers to teach them, and thereby started the first modern universities, then I know what kids could be if we let them. Yes, the times were very different. Yet, the two following excerpts from former students reveal anew the possibilities of youth today. They just need the right environment and plenty of encouragement.

The first is from a government course evaluation. Students were asked to tell what was most valuable to them in the course and offer suggestions for change. This student understood so well the Grow/Learn System.

> General concepts definitely overrode nitty-gritty facts, and thinking is more important than knowing. I have felt this way for a long time, but this is the first class that has let me put it into practice. Most valuable were: work on and discussion of [political theory]; the short time we spent on comparative politics; conflicts in civil rights and liberties; a perfect way to end the year—discussion of the 'good society' and morality . . . I don't think you should change anything, but I know there's lots of things you would like to change that are beyond your control (time restrictions, unmotivated students, administration policy). For me, your class was as close to ideal as I think South Lakes can get. But I don't know, if I was conservative by nature, you may have scared me stiff. I hope not. I know that's the last thing you would want, but still you are an authority figure. I'm not saying give up your own positions, and I don't think you can give up any more authority than you already have, but maybe just tame the rage. I myself like the excitement of your character as it is; maybe that's why people take Mr. Tripp's class to begin with

. . . Oh, I almost forgot, the map tests were stupid, but I see their purpose . . . I am leaving this class with a lot more questions than answers; its a strange but satisfying feeling. You have opened my eyes to much more substance for questioning. I am leaving with frustration with our government and with a vision of room for change. Keep fighting, Mr. Tripp.

The second excerpt is from the alumni survey of Shashin Singh, a 1988 South Lakes graduate. Shashin's perception leaped out at me from the page like a beautiful shaft of light. This is his response to the question about his most valuable academic experiences in high school:

> It is a valuable academic experience when you see a teacher come everyday in a school year bringing enthusiasm to their job. You see that the teacher wants to be there and is not there just for the job. The teachers want to teach and believe me the students know who these teachers are. I think that this translates to the students by way of seeing the joy in learning. Something good comes from seeing such practices on a daily basis. I think that seeing someone do what they love to do (for some, teaching) is more important than having someone who is an expert on a subject. A good teacher will open their students to the possibilities of a subject . . . I guess having a few good teachers inspired my most valuable academic experience in high school.

This is Shashin's response to the question about his best learning situations in high school:

> The situation that I respond best to is when I am challenged to discover new material and incorporate that material with what I already know. That way, I learn the material in a way that is unique to how I relate to things. Still, this forces me to look at things from a different perspective and to either enlarge or take into consideration this new view. This often causes me to change my thoughts on subjects and sometimes actually will enhance a subject by giving it a greater depth of understanding.

* * *

Bless them all.